The Judgment of Jonah

THE FOLLOWING BOOKS BY JACQUES ELLUL
ARE AVAILABLE IN ENGLISH

The Theological Foundation of Law (1960; 1969)

The Technological Society (1964)

Propaganda (1966)

The Political Illusion (1967)

A Critique of the New Commonplaces (1968)

The Presence of the Kingdom (1967)

Violence: Reflections from a Christian Perspective (1969)

To Will and To Do (1969)

The Meaning of the City (1970)

Prayer and Modern Man (1970)

The Judgment of Jonah (1971)

The Judgment of Jonah

by

Jacques Ellul

Translated by Geoffrey W. Bromiley

WILLIAM B. EERDMANS PUBLISHING COMPANY
Grand Rapids, Michigan

Copyright © 1971 by William B. Eerdmans Publishing Company

Library of Congress Catalog Card Number: 70-142901
ISBN 0-8028-1373-9
Printed in the United States of America

Translated from the French *Le Livre de Jonas,*
Cahiers Bibliques de Foi et Vie, Paris

First printing, May 1971
Second printing, August 1974

Translator's Preface

Another book on Jonah might seem to need some explanation or justification, but not so when the author is Jacques Ellul. The lively mind and ready pen of this important theologian are a sufficient vindication in themselves.

This is not, of course, a commentary in the traditional sense. A few matters of history, date, and composition are briefly touched on in the Introduction. Here and there one also finds some linguistic discussion. But the work is not scientific exegesis. Its value lies elsewhere.

One might call it an existential commentary. An important aim of the author is to bring out the relevance of the story, of the person, mission and situation of Jonah, to Christians in our own time. Some of the suggestions may be rather forced or fanciful, and they are not all self-consistent, but the power and essential truth of the application will hardly be questioned.

But above all, this is a theological or more specifically a christological commentary. The author's chief aim is to relate the book, not to Christians, but to Christ. Ellul thinks Christ is the center of all Scripture and he also takes seriously the specific reference which Christ makes to the sign of Jonah. If this reading is correct and the Bible is indeed a unity, the exposition of Ellul, though not developed in detail, has a distinctive theological contribution to make.

Naturally those who want other questions settled will not be pleased or satisfied. But those who want acute theological insight and are not afraid of plain, hard-hitting application will read this vivid study with relish and profit.

Geoffrey W. Bromiley

Pasadena, California

Contents

Introduction

It is easy not to take the little story of Jonah seriously. We all remember that it has been one of the favorite targets of criticism of the Bible, and Voltaire took delight in scoffing at its improbabilities. There can be no doubt that one remains uneasy as to the reality of some of the facts recorded in the text.

The story of the fish is undoubtedly difficult to accept. The most fantastic of explanations have been offered (a ship of this name, a mistake on Jonah's part, etc.), but the brute fact is itself inexplicable. It is no obstacle to faith, for one can always invoke a miracle. But with some rare exceptions (the miracles of Elisha) the Bible itself teaches prudence in relation to apparently gratuitous acts of this kind. It is patent that the miracle would be of a different quality from those worked by Jesus and would be much closer to the dubious miracles of the Acta Sanctorum. To be sure, nothing is impossible with God. But it is also possible that if we take this view the teaching derived from the miracle would be less profound and authentic than if we were to regard the story as the account, not of a material miracle, but of a spiritual adventure. Some of the details about Nineveh also cause difficulty, e.g., that it was a three days' march across the city. Nineveh was certainly big, but was it this big? Nor is there any account of the conversion of Nineveh in the history of the city. If such a city was converted—and the text seems to imply an authentic conversion and not just one that was temporary or feigned—then one might expect that history would have kept some trace of it in the form of legends or statues.

Other problems might be mentioned, but one should especially emphasize the affinity of the first part of the story with other legends. Almost everywhere, from Finland to Canada, one finds the account of the divinely sent hero who was swallowed by a great fish, and then thrown up by a sovereign act of God. Whether this be a solar myth or a legend common to mankind, it does not put the story of Jonah in too good a light.

Then many scholars date the work late, between 400 and 190 B.C., after the destruction of Nineveh, so that if the story is about Jonah the son of Amittai it comes from four or five centuries after he lived, according to this view.

In face of these difficulties, which are the more moderate ones, there are two traditional positions. The first is a literalism which closes its ears to the critics almost to the point of *credo quia absurdum*. The danger here is that of attaching faith to a record rather than to Jesus Christ. For the true reality of the book is Jesus Christ and to divert our faith from him to facts which are not so significant in themselves can be a serious mistake.

The second position is that mostly adopted by historians. The book is part of the Haggadic stream. It is a moral and religious tale designed to teach certain ideas to the Jewish people. It is thus a work of imagination, perhaps founded on a primitive legend. It is a spiritual satire directed against the narrow particularism of some Jews who are offended at God's patience with pagan nations. There is, however, a serious obstacle to this interpretation, as also to the more radical one of a simple legend. Jonah is in the canon. If it was just a simple tale like the many other pious stories abroad among the Jews in the 3rd century, one can hardly think it would have made its way into the canon. For the Jews were difficult and stingy when it came to regarding a work as a revelation. Furthermore, if this book is a satire on particularism, the improbability of this whole position strikes the eye at once. One has only to recall the seriousness and depth of rabbinic exegesis to know for certain that the work goes much beyond this.

It does not appear that the story is just a parable or

apology, or that its contents are just moralizing and edifying. The Jews had many works of this kind which they never thought of regarding as canonical.

On the other hand, by placing it in the canon the Jews did not provide for it a criterion of authentic historicity. They did not place it among the historical books but among the prophetic books. They did not seek in it information about the life of one of their prophets but instruction which is singularly profound and complex.

We have here, not moral ideas, but teaching about man's relations with God and God's dealings with man. That is to say, it is in very truth a revelation.

* * * * *

The second fact to be considered is that the Jews classed the book among the prophetic writings. Now this is not evidently a prophetic book in the sense the Jews could understand. The prophetic books have clear-cut characteristics. They do not usually tell the story of the prophet. But the prophet is a living, concrete figure, and his prophecies and teachings are always concrete, apart from the final section of Isaiah. They relate to specific historical facts and situations. The prophet's teachings and commands are not general in character. They are given explicitly in a way which is direct and positive. The prophet plainly declares God's will in a given situation. Finally, the prophet's message is addressed to Israel. Only God's people seem capable of hearing God's word.

The Book of Jonah is quite different. In this respect it recalls the records of Elijah and Elisha, though these do not occur in the prophets but in the historical books. In the story of Jonah the important thing is the life of this man, his controversy with God, in distinction from other books which are intentionally reticent about the personal relation of the prophet to God. The primary thing here is a biographical fact (no matter whether authentic or not) rather than a word of God to the prophet. Jonah is not even shown to be a qualified prophet. He is given a mission, but

11

only from Kings do we know his qualifications. This again is exceptional as compared with the other prophetic books.

The story is no less strange from another angle. God's word here does not relate to a historical situation. This is the strongest point in favor of a Haggadic interpretation: the book is not a true prophetic book because it is not connected with a precise epoch in Israel's history but gives general instruction; Jonah is not bound to the life of his people here, and since we know that he was in fact, the book is not true prophecy.

Another difference from the other prophets is that the message is not addressed to the people of Israel. What Jonah receives from God to say to men is a word for Nineveh. Now there are undoubtedly prophecies addressed to Tyre, Sidon and Egypt, but these are prophecies within Israel and ultimately for this people; they are sayings about Tyre, Sidon, etc., but sayings received by the chosen people. Here the word is spoken to Nineveh and for Nineveh. There is no question of Israel, and this seems very singular since all the prophets are closely bound to the people of Israel, being there on behalf of the people to bring it to God. The prophet cannot think of himself in abstraction from the elect people. Jonah, in contrast, seems to bear no relation to the elect people.

One might say that it is not the word which God addresses to Jonah, but his adventures which are a kind of lesson or experience that God gives to his people. But this does not convey at all the distinctive aspect of the book.

There is a final difference directly connected with the preceding one. All the prophets, when addressing the people of Israel, take the covenant between God and his people as their basis. It is there that they find the point of their argument. It is from this starting-point that a word of God becomes prophecy. But for Jonah, as it is not a question of the people, so it is not a question of the covenant. If a word of God is spoken, it does not rest on

12

the free act by which God binds himself to his people. On the contrary, this book seems to take up again the very ancient idea of a god bound by nature to a people and a specific territory without annexing to the bond any promises.

The problem thus arises why the Book of Jonah was admitted to the prophetic writings when in form and genre there seems to be nothing to qualify it for this. The view has been advanced that the decision is based on the contents of the book. There are in the story general ideas like the general ideas of the prophets.

One finds, for example, the idea of an omnipotent and unique God, not bound to a specific land, but the God of the universe whom nothing can escape. One finds the idea of a God who threatens but whose threats are not unconditional, who is in relation to men and accepts their repentance. One finds the notion of universalism which takes up again the first two ideas. Hence it may be said that if the story relates to the people of Nineveh it is because the author is concerned about foreign nations. He wants to show that God is God of pagans too, not just for their condemnation, not just in terms of his power, but for their salvation as well. On this view the first part of the book is a polemic against Israelites who do not want to go abroad to proclaim salvation to others and who think that other nations should simply be condemned. The aim of the second part is to declare the divine pardon to the world through preaching and repentance.

It may be noted that this places the book quite definitely at a time when believing Jews were offended at God's patience with nations which oppressed his people. These Jews were awaiting the fulfilment of the prophecies of the exile. Haggai and Zechariah, for example, had promised the destruction of Babylon and the shattering of pagan empires as a condition of Israel's salvation. The book is written against this view. It advances a position of higher spirituality and its ideas are related to the higher message of Jeremiah and Isaiah. This would show why the book was listed among the prophets. Within the current of prophetic ideas, it is a correction of earlier prophets in terms of the great ones. But unfortunately the whole of this theory rests on modern notions. Prophetism was not a current of ideas. To talk of a prophetic doctrine is to talk like a 20th century intellectual. The prophet is characterized, not by ideas, but by the fact that God's word is addressed to him and is to be conveyed by him. The content of this word of God may vary according to situation and the divine decision without affecting faith. Conversely, saying the same things as a divine revelation is not *ipso facto* a word of God. The Jews do not have a rational view of prophecy but a view according to faith. The important thing in recognizing prophecy is to know from whom the word comes, not what it contains. To rationalize dogmatically is to have a completely false perspective on the text and on the reasons the Jews might have for accepting it in the way they do. The text emphatically does not present ideas nor a doctrine about God. It is the history of a relation between man and God, and it has been accepted by the chosen people as a prophetic word of God.

* * * * *

This raises again the whole question why Israel recognized it as prophecy when there were so many reasons against this. If we take the word "prophecy" seriously, we are obliged to see that there is only one reason why Israel accepted this book as such, and this is the inspiration of the Holy Spirit. Obviously it is no extraordinary discovery to admit the inspiration of Scripture. The extraordinary thing is that we are led to admit it by a kind of human reason.

The Jews did not recognize the book as prophecy because it had the same characteristics as other prophetic books but for mysterious reasons which they did not fully

14

grasp themselves and which we today can decipher. At this point they were led to bear witness precisely against themselves, though in the last resort this was good news for them too.

As Christians we normally allow that prophetic writings are such by relation to Jesus Christ; on the other hand the Jews could allow them to be such not because they announced the Messiah but because they conveyed God's judgment here and now on the elect people, because they were God's word fashioned for his people and relating to its history. On this basis a prophetic book is not symbolic. The prophet may perform symbolic acts like Ezekiel, but the book itself does not contain symbol. Prophecy does not proceed in this indirect way in its books. In this respect it differs from the historical books. And this is also another point of difference as compared with the Book of Jonah.

Finally, the two aspects of prophecy noted (word of God to Israel and intimation of Christ) are not absolutely connected with one another nor necessarily conjoined. In other words, the books have their own signification apart from any intimation of Jesus Christ. They may be self-sufficient even though they derive their true reference from Jesus Christ and prophetic fulfilment. The patent meaning does not have to lead to the second meaning, nor does the latter necessarily qualify the former.

Now this is not quite true in relation to Jonah. If we look narrowly for what it says to the chosen people quite apart from any other consideration, we see that it is not prophecy and that its signification is slight. If we want to find out why it is prophetic, we are obliged to refer to Jesus Christ. Apart from him it is impossible to find a prophetic sense in its symbols (which are not allegories). The great difficulty in interpreting the book is that the symbols do not have a single sense and one has to try to take them in their totality. It is a generally acknowledged fact that a biblical text may quite legitimately have several senses, and that so far as possible we ought to view these various senses globally.

Along these lines Jonah, or more precisely the relation between Jonah and God, is representative of the history of Israel. In some sense Jonah is Israel, not just because he is a member of the people but because his situation is that of the chosen people itself. This alone, however, is not enough. One part of the book cannot really be understood in this way, namely, the entry into death and hell. This makes sense only if we think of Israel as dependent on and bound to the one who truly enters into death and hell. Without this, we are obliged to regard all this side of it as an exaggeration of oriental poetry.

Nevertheless, it is incontestable that Jonah represents to the chosen people its constant relation to God, namely, its constant disobedience and the pardon which it receives through the condemnation inflicted by other nations as agents of God's judgment with a view to the salvation of Israel. This gives an absolute and permanent dimension to what the facts of Jewish history continually record in detail. But just because we have here a kind of objective revelation, we cannot receive it in isolation. It would be a message of despair if it were not accompanied by the objective revelation of the permanent presence of God's salvation.

It may be noted as well that to the degree that Jonah represents Israel he also represents for us the new Israel, the Church, whose relations with God are still of the same type as those of ancient Israel.

Secondly, the book concerns all men. It records the attitude of all men when they receive God's call and are in the presence of his grace. In this sense, too, it is prophetic. It is not just a general word. It is a specific word relating to all of us. Once again, however, this word is not wholly true if it simply documents the irreconcilable opposition between man and God, closing with .an almost ironical lesson which God gave to this man who was debating between nature and grace. It is not a full prophecy relating to us unless the situation has an outcome, holds a truth of life. As a mere record of fact it is nothing. But as a record of fact which leads up to an eternal and unique relation between God and man it is of full significance for all men. We shall have to take up this point throughout our exposition, but briefly this is why the prophecy about Israel and man presupposes Jesus Christ if the Book of Jonah is to make sense. This prophecy does not blot out the others; it confirms and elucidates them, and gives the book its full value.

Jonah is a figure, a type of Christ. To prove this one has only to consider that Jesus referred the revelation of Jonah to himself. But many of the details also confirm it. We do not have only a general figure. The situations in which Jonah found himself are situations of the Messiah. Naturally Jonah is not Christ. He is a man. But he is placed by God in circumstances like those in which Jesus Christ found himself. This will be made plain later.

If one rejects this sense, there is no other. Apart from it the Jews committed a serious act of folly in adopting the book as a canonical and prophetic book. For its prophecy about Israel and man, taken alone, is of absurd banality and impossible to accept. It becomes true, full and acceptable only if Jonah intimates the Messiah. Only in this light can one understand the other prophecies. This is why we say that the Jews did not really know what they were doing when they accepted the book as prophetic. The Holy Spirit knew on their behalf.

This leads to two conclusions. The first is that whether or not the book is historical is of secondary importance, for the story finds its true value not in itself, in what it is, but in what it denotes. Its relevance derives from the truth which it embodies, from the one who fulfills the prophecy. The prophecy is authentic only if what it denotes is fulfilled. Even if the scribes and doctors do use legends common to all peoples, or "Haggadah," to transmit what

17

the Holy Spirit reveals to them, this is not of primary importance so long as the word of God is faithfully transmitted, so long as the prophecy becomes truth through him who fulfills it. Apart from him any sacred word is a human word and through him even a legend may carry truth. God is free to choose his own means.

The second conclusion is that one must take the Book of Jonah for what it is: a prophetic book. A commentary must respect this character and indeed takes it as its center. Hence one is not to interpret the text in a moral sense, in the sense of edification or piety, or in an ecclesiological sense, as Herbert Werner does (1950) in a work which is interesting but seems to miss the point because it neglects the prophetic aspect. This does not mean that the work has no edifying or ecclesiological value; it means that any such value derives from its central character. It is by relating the specific revelations of the book to its central revelation that we ourselves shall try to understand it.

The Word of the Lord Came to Jonah

Now the word of the Lord came to Jonah the son of Amittai, saying, "Arise, go to Nineveh, that great city, and cry against it; for their wickedness has come up before me." But Jonah rose to flee to Tarshish from the presence of the Lord. He went down to Joppa and found a ship going to Tarshish; so he paid the fare, and went on board, to go with them to Tarshish, away from the presence of the Lord.

But the Lord hurled a great wind upon the sea, and there was a mighty tempest on the sea, so that the ship threatened to break up. Then the mariners were afraid, and each cried to his god; and they threw the wares that were in the ship into the sea, to lighten it for them. But Jonah had gone down into the inner part of the ship and had lain down, and was fast asleep. So the captain came and said to him, "What do you mean, you sleeper? Arise, call upon your god! Perhaps the god will give a thought to us, that we do not perish."

And they said to one another, "Come, let us cast lots, that we may know on whose account this evil has come upon us." So they cast lots, and the lot fell upon Jonah. Then they said to him, "Tell us, on whose account this evil has come upon us? What is your occupation? And whence do you come? What is your country? And of what people are you?" And he said to them, "I am a Hebrew; and I fear the Lord, the God of heaven, who made the sea and the dry land." Then the men were exceedingly afraid, and said to him, "What is this that you have done!" For the men knew that he was fleeing from the presence of the Lord, because he had told them.

Then they said to him, "What shall we do to you, that the sea may quiet down for us?" For the sea grew more and more tempestuous. He said to them, "Take me up and throw me into the sea; then the sea will quiet down for you; for I know it is because of me that this great tempest has come upon us." Nevertheless the men rowed hard to bring the ship back to land, but they could not, for the sea grew more and more tempestuous against them. Therefore they cried to the Lord, "We beseech thee, O Lord, let us not perish for this man's life, and lay not on us innocent blood; for thou, O Lord, hast done as it pleased thee." So they took up Jonah and threw him into the sea; and the sea ceased from its raging. Then the men feared the Lord exceedingly, and they offered a sacrifice to the Lord and made vows.

1. THE ELECTION

Jonah is chosen by God to take his word to Nineveh. The text does not say what reasons led God to make this choice. They were certainly not human reasons. The rest of the story shows that Jonah was not specifically qualified for the work by character, piety, or virtues. Everything begins the moment God decides to choose. We are not to go beyond this in an effort to know God's reasons or hidden counsel. We can begin to apprehend only from the moment when a relation is set up between God and us, when he reveals his decision concerning us. The story begins when the word of God is revealed to Jonah.

We usually translate: "The word of the Lord came to . . . ," but in fact the Hebrew simply says "is." The word of God is. It is for Jonah and to him. This shows clearly that the word is not just words. It is not the phrases God speaks. It is a power which exists and manifests itself. This is why, when the word is thus revealed to a man, he is not at all in the situation we always imagine: a subordinate receiving orders from a superior; a subordinate who ought to fulfill the order, though this is just a collection of words, which certainly aims at action, and is backed by social sanctions, but which is not itself an action so that in large measure the subordinate is free: he may obey or disobey. The word of God, however, is not at all like this. It is power and not just discourse. It transforms what it touches. It cannot be anything but creative and salvific. It never fails to take effect. A human order, when not obeyed, is without effect, but God's word always attains its end. In fact this is one of the main lessons of the Book of Jonah. The word effects God's decision after all kinds of detours and complications which arise because God takes into account and respects man's decisions too.

When the word intervenes in a situation, it changes that situation. When it comes on a man, it changes that man even if he refuses to listen. This goes beyond mere obedience. The word enlists man in an adventure into which he carries all those around him and which may be a controversy with God.

This word is addressed to an individual man. In effect it is always specific. It is not a general truth which any man might grasp and understand with no particular action on God's part. God is first the God of an individual man. Election and vocation relate to an individual and not a crowd, not mankind, not man in general.

We know nothing about the one thus chosen and designated. The Bible does not think it necessary to give us this information. We know almost nothing about Jonah, his family, village, or person. He begins to be important only when the word of the Lord is on him. He becomes personal at this moment. Before he no doubt had the worth of any man. He was an individual. Perhaps he was very important. But his destiny was fixed. He was subject to destiny. Now he is taken from the ranks. He achieves singularity. He masters destiny. He is called to change history for himself and others.

This does not imply individualism. Jonah is a member of the chosen people. The word he is given is part of the covenant. Jonah belongs to the people of God and this word itself integrates him the more closely into the people of God. Throughout his adventure he is alone: alone in face of God and in face of death and in face of Nineveh. But in his solitude, whether aware of it or not, he belongs to the cloud of witnesses, to the 7,000 men who have not bowed the knee to Baal, to the remnant of Israel. In fact Jonah represents the whole people of Israel, and if he is quite alone he still represents the whole people, both Israel and the Church. This is why God cannot rest content with his individual and arbitrary decision. When Jonah turns his back and flees, it is not just Jonah who is at stake but the whole Church and the world. God cannot let him go. If this man is not independent of God it is because of the world to which he is sent.

* * * * *

The word had only to come to Jonah for his situation to be genuinely and totally changed even though he himself was not yet changed. What was it that changed, according to the text?

We note first that this word which manifests God's choice or election is not just an intimation of this election. It is not a kind of announcement which makes known God's decision and which contributes to our personal satisfaction, our personal joy, our edification, and our peace. This word makes known to Jonah that he has been chosen for a purpose. God's election is never a choice which stops with the choice. When God picks out a man and speaks to him, it is to engage him in a work, an action. Nowhere in Scripture do we find indeterminate or purely mystical vocation. Nowhere do we find general election, i.e., election to be a Christian *grosso modo,* to fulfill the will of God at large. When God addresses a man he does not merely give singularity to the man; he also particularizes his will for him. There is, of course, a general will of God which in some sort applies to all of us. But election does not consist in knowledge of this general will. It is enlistment in a precise action, a specific work. If God chooses a man, it is in order that he may serve in the work God has undertaken. It is in the measure that he does serve thus that his true election is made known and that it becomes more clear and certain for him. We cannot be content, then, with Christian virtues; vocation presupposes taking part in the work. There is no election apart from taking part in this way.

Moreover, when God has chosen a man who has a function to discharge, he never goes back on this. The man who is thus enlisted willy-nilly in God's action remains a chosen man even though he refuses and flees. The fact that Jonah flees is by no means unique. On the contrary, one might say that all men, when they become aware of this call, begin by refusing and fleeing. But God's choice persists. He has chosen for a precise action, and so long as this is not performed God pursues man. This is true of all the men of the Bible, including Jonah.

In reality (spiritual reality) it is much too simple to think that God offers his grace to man and man accepts or refuses. When God has graciously chosen a man his grace continues even though the man does not do what God has decided. On the other hand, this persistence of election, of which Jonah is an extraordinary example (and which is connected with the fact that God chooses for a specific action), does not entail a negation of man's will. God pursues this man, conducts him through his whole life, in order to bring about the consent of this man's will to what God has decided. We will see later the details of God's dealings with Jonah.

On each occasion man can refuse and on each occasion God begins again until man has finally chosen to accept. It may thus be said that by this word man is both more free and also less free than in the presence of a human order. He is more free because he is detached by this word even from social contingencies; he must break with the world. This is what we find with Jonah. No matter whether he decides to obey or to flee, there is a rupture with his daily life, his background, his country. Henceforth he is separated from others. The matter is so important that everything which previously shaped the life of this man humanly and sociologically fades from the scene. He is in a situation such as no human order could present to him. Anything that might impel him to obey according to the world has lost its value and weight for him. But he is also enlisted in an action which he has not chosen and cannot avoid. He is pursued by a devouring love which wants him

24

totally, in the ardor of his own converted heart. He is pursued by an unwearying patience which will use every means to bring it about finally that this man yields to God's reason. And the adventure in which man is obliged to stake everything in a freedom which is given, but given only for this adventure, seems to be extraordinarily important for God. In some sense God engages himself in the work in which he engages man.

There is another aspect of this situation in which the word of God sets man and which may be seen in the story. Everything circles around the man who has been chosen. A tempest is unleashed. This is a natural event and science can explain its causes and consequences. We can accept this attitude quite well. When we have spoken of electricity and atmospheric depressions, we can stop and realize that there is no other cause behind these causes. But Jonah teaches us that this storm, whose physical causes are the same as those of all other storms, is there only for Jonah and because of Jonah. It has other effects. It sweeps the coasts, disperses fish, causes ships to founder. But its purpose is to smash inflexible Jonah. Thus the elements and many men, especially the sailors, are engaged in the adventure of Jonah with him and because of him. One sees here the weight and seriousness of vocation. God thinks his choice so important, and takes the one elected so seriously, that he brings nature into play to see that this man fulfills his vocation.

This does not mean that we have to inquire into the spiritual meaning of every event. But we have to realize that these events, in spite of their rational appearance, are in effect part of the formidable accomplishment of the work of God. This is not supplementary or additional to the wholly natural history of nature and the world. This history, which it is easy enough to explain rationally, is simply an instrument of God's work.

Among these events there is perhaps one which takes place because of us. We must not try to puzzle out which one. It is always the one which we do not recognize at first. In face of the tempest, Jonah sleeps.

2. MAN'S ATTITUDE

In this history into which Jonah is now launched we find two types of men, Jonah and the sailors.

When Jonah hears the word which comes to him he refuses to obey it. He has every reason to refuse from the human standpoint. It is veritable folly to go to Nineveh, that great city which was always in arms against God and his people. To begin with, he would have to make a tremendous journey across the desert: about 750 miles on foot. This was the first difficulty. Then he would arrive at a very large city with far more than 120,000 inhabitants, and he would be quite alone there. Imagine today a lone individual setting off unaided to preach the word to such a city! Even if it had been christianized, imagine a lone individual undertaking to preach the word with no "sociological structure" in Paris or Berlin! Individuals have in fact tried to confront and stir large cities, from Cleomenes in Alexandria to Garry Davis in Paris, and we know only too well with what results.

Again, the mission is to be to the Ninevites. This people was a traditional foe of Israel. The age of Jonah was the zenith of Assyrian power. Between 750 and 700 was the time when Damascus was captured, when Samaria was conquered, when Judah was ravaged, when the kingdom of Israel was subjugated during the reign of Jehu. The kingdom of Israel where Jonah lived was an Assyrian province. It was from there that Jehovah was sending a man to preach repentance to the conquerors. Imagine a Frenchman going to preach repentance to Berlin in 1941 or 1942! The people to whom Jonah was to preach was the most martial, the most realistic, and the most cruel people of antiquity. It was the people which scorched its enemies alive to decorate its walls and pyramids with their skin.

26

Moreover, one must put the word Nineveh in its biblical perspective. Like Babylon, Nineveh was the place of man's omnipotence. It was man's counter-creation confronting God's creation. It was the place of human pride which allies itself with demons and rejects God. It was the world fast closed against God. Spiritually this was what Nineveh represented. Opposed to God, this city was necessarily opposed to his people. If there was constant war between Nineveh and the two kingdoms, this was no accident of history. It was the predetermination of forces. The drama is thus much more profound. God orders Jonah to go to the very place he could not go—a light among the darkness. In sum, Nineveh is the "world" in the theological sense.

When we grasp the order in its historical context or spiritual sense, we run up against the same difficulty, the same challenge. God is asking the impossible from Jonah. And we have to realize that what God asks is always impossible from the human standpoint and according to man's judgment. Jonah had good reason to refuse and flee.

Anything is better than certain death at Nineveh. Jonah will not accept the impossible from God. He judges as the world judges. But he does not take into account the fact that he is engaged in an adventure in which it is no longer possible to judge thus and that decisions taken according to the reasoning of the world will lead nowhere and solve nothing.

He embarks for Tarshish, probably Tartessus, a town in Spain. He sets off in a direction which is the precise opposite of that indicated by God. He can no longer live his life where he is. He must leave, and do so as a fugitive. He flees, the text says. He has a bad conscience and flees like Adam and Cain. He knows that there is no justice for him and that the only solution is to put a barrier between himself and God. He flees "away from the presence of the Lord." Historians say that this statement goes back to an age when the gods were local. The God of Israel was localized in the territory occupied by Israel, and to leave

27

this territory was to escape God's power. This supposedly explains the material departure of Jonah. Having received an order he cannot execute, he goes abroad where there are other gods which have not given the order. But this explanation hardly seems acceptable to me. Even by 750 B.C. Judaism had strongly affirmed the idea that Yahweh is a universal God, and how much more so by 305 B.C. when the text was supposedly edited! Furthermore, verse 9 shows that Jonah knew perfectly well that Yahweh is a God who owns the whole earth. One might say, then, that the text is aimed polemically against any who believed in a local god, but this no longer applied by 350. It was no longer a problem.

It seems to me that the real sense here is spiritual. In departing, Jonah breaks with the people which God has chosen. He no longer wants to belong to the chosen people. He prefers to follow other gods (for he knows indeed that there are other gods where he is going) rather than the living God. He snaps all that which humanly binds him to this living God, thinking it enough to fling his will, his refusal, in the face of God to end the whole affair. He chooses to damn himself. This is the meaning of fleeing from the face of the Lord. It seems preferable to obedience, so impossible is the order. To achieve damnation he pays. He pays his passage. The story of Jonah is indeed the story of all of us. What sacrifices are we not ready to make to be far from the face of God, unable as we are to accept that it is God himself who fulfills his impossible will!

A final aspect of the attitude of Jonah is that during the storm he goes down into the interior of the ship and sleeps. This has been explained in various ways. Some say it is a sign Jonah had a good conscience; he was convinced he was doing what he had to do. Others suggest he was only feigning sleep.

To me, however, it seems that this detail is very clear if we take it with all that precedes. Jonah flees from the presence of God and during the tempest he sleeps. The point is that he refuses even to contemplate this storm. He refuses to see it except as a natural phenomenon about which he can do nothing. He will not see in it God's act, God's appeal, God's pointer. He prefers to know nothing about it. He continues to flee by plunging into unconsciousness in order not to know that it comes from God.

This detail, however, must also be set in relation to what follows. Jonah is roused out of sleep by the sailors, who call him and make him come. His sleep was also a refusal to accept solidarity with them, with their material and spiritual destiny.

When all the world is in danger, the man who flees from the word of God seals himself off in his solitude, willing neither to see nor to hear anything of what others are doing. His destiny is no longer their destiny. He sleeps.

We thus have various reactions of man when God's election has been revealed to him. The reactions are not just those of Jonah.

* * * * *

With Jonah are the sailors. Without knowing it they are involved in a curious history. These Joppa sailors do not belong to the Jewish people. They are pagans, or, in modern terms, non-Christians. But they have set sail with a member of the chosen people, a Christian. The lot of non-Christians and Christians is henceforth linked; they are in the same boat. The safety of all depends on what each does. But each has his own thing to do. They are in the same storm, subject to the same peril, and they want the same outcome. They are in a unique enterprise, and this ship typifies our situation. What do these sailors do? First, they do all they humanly can; while Jonah sleeps, they try all human methods to save the vessel, to keep the enterprise going (v. 5). What experience, nautical science, reason, and common sense teach them to do, they do. In this sense they do their duty. The sailors are in charge of the world, and in normal conditions they discharge their task correctly. We can ask no more of them. The tragic thing here, however, is that if conditions cease to be normal, it is not the fault of the sailors, the pagans; it is the fault of the Christian who has sailed with them. It is because of him that the situation is such that the knowledge and tradition of the sailors can do no more. We have to realize once again that this is how it usually is with the world; the storm is unleashed because of the unfaithfulness of the Church and Christians. This being so, if the tempest is God's will to constrain his Church, a will by which the whole human enterprise is endangered, one can easily see why man's technical devices are of no avail.

Recognizing more or less vaguely the presence of spiritual forces, the sailors try next to approach them. As each knows best (v. 5) they beseech their gods, both good and evil. No doubt they also put their trust in "the dialectical meaning of history" and "progress" among these different gods. What else can they do, seeing they do not know the true God? They also turn to obscure powers, magic. They draw lots. After all, this recourse (which proves to be effective and in God's hands, since the result is right) is no less natural to man. If the sailors do not know that drawing lots is forbidden by the God of Israel, this is because Israel has not made known to them who is in truth its God. It is because Israel has not discharged its mission. Why do we Christians complain about the way the world acts when it depends on us whether the world is set before the Savior's cross? Obviously, if the sailors had known the divine prohibition and continued to use magic, this would have been open to condemnation. In the present case, however, God uses these wretched human devices too.

Then the sailors address Jonah. Non-Christians address Christians, not because they accord them the least superiority or even the least value. Jonah, like Christians, is asleep. But after all, each is calling on his god, and why should not they be invited to do so as well? Even if it does no good, in the common emergency non-Christians cannot (with good reason) accept that any should separate themselves or hide or remain indifferent to their efforts. Perhaps non-Christians do not expect much of Christians. But at all events they rouse them and force them to have a part in the drama. They rouse them, i.e., they make Christians see what is really going on. A remarkable thing about even the active Christian is that he never has much more than a vague idea about reality. He is lost in the slumber of his activities, his good works, his chorales, his theology, his evangelizing, his communities. He always skirts reality. He views the storm from outside, not as one who is in the boat, even if his intentions, unlike Jonah's, are good. It is non-Christians who have to waken him out of his sleep to share actively the common lot. Again we have a current situation. It is National Socialism and Communism that have roused and still rouse the Church. "Call upon your god! Perhaps the god will give a thought to us." Not without a note of scorn does the pagan address the useless Church, but he must not miss any chances. To be sure, this is not faith, but it is at least an experiment. The world puts God and the Christian to the test when it needs to, and this test knots the drama around Christians. They no longer have any right to go away, to refuse. They are intentionally involved by non-Christians, and God uses non-Christians to this end.

When Jonah recognizes his responsibility, when he sees his guilt, when he realizes he ought to be for these non-Christians, for the world, when Christians and the Church confess the totality of their faith, the result is a series of astonishing facts. But this attitude on the part of Christians cannot be just verbal. Jonah does not make speeches. He lets himself be put in question in the totality of his life; it is a life and death matter. He is ready to be completely condemned for his unfaithfulness and to lose his life. He thus becomes the witness, the martyr. This is what is really needed. When the Church is ready to play its part in the world's adventure—and this is why it is sent—it is neither the power which organizes and dominates the world nor the organization which makes speeches and does good works; it is the mother of martyrs, of those who, accepting God's condemnation, sacrifice their life in order that the world may come through the drama.

With this the drama does in fact reach its denouement. The sea calms down and the pagans are converted. The sailors are gripped by a great fear of the omnipotent God who manifests both his patience and his justice, both his power and his kindness. To be sure, they have not received a revelation of God's love. To be sure, they do not yet worship him as the only true God. But they do penetrate to the fear of the Lord, and we know the important role this played in the faith of Israel. It is not terror. We should not forget that in Psalm 130 God pardons in order that we may fear him. This fear comes from accomplished grace. The condemned man who is pardoned is seized by fear at the power which has caused death to retreat.

The sailors are led by this fear to put themselves in the hands of this God. They make offerings and vows. This is a consecration of their possessions and persons. Snatched from death by so great a miracle, the pagans in turn consent to the consecration which was total in Jonah. After the martyr, those who believe, not because of the martyr but because of the manifested power of God, give their lives to God who rolls back tempests. The story of the sailors ends here. They cannot go further except as their faith develops.

3. GOD'S STRATEGY

The story brings out a remarkable aspect of the strategy which God patiently follows in the world.

God has chosen Jonah to be the bearer of his grace and salvation. Jonah refuses. What does God do? Does he reject, damn, and smite him? Does he force him, not respecting his will but taking him unwillingly to Nineveh and making him speak against his wishes? Does he accept

Jonah's decision and let him go his own way? These are human decisions which in our simplicity we often attribute to God. God's action is infinitely more subtle and complex. God is personally involved in this adventure. He is no *deus ex machina.* He takes part in the drama. He is not just the omnipotent God doing as he wills in heaven and earth. He stoops to man's loftiness. As he wrestled with Jacob at the ford of Jabbok, so he wrestles as an equal with Jonah.

He first uses existing factors, e.g., what we should call mechanical solidarity. Jonah is in solidarity with the sailors. This solidarity becomes tighter and fuller as the situation becomes more dangerous. Then he uses Jonah's faith. This is no great thing. It is in no sense triumphant. It is little more than knowledge. The pagans do not know what the adventure is all about. Jonah does. He has the key to the riddle. Christians share the same knowledge. This is about their only difference from non-Christians. But the trouble, the great trouble, is that this knowledge results in self-accusation. Jonah is led to this. He has understood God's action. He realizes that it is his own condemnation. He understands it because he has been chosen by God. This shows us on the one side that his sleep was no sign of a good conscience and on the other that he has known for a long time what life in God is. Thus when God sets the solidarity plainly before him he counts on the fact that Jonah is still in the faith. He begins there. He confronts Jonah with his responsibilities. He impales him on the horns of a dilemma. According to Scripture this is often God's way with man. He forces on him an ineluctable choice: Either . . . or. Man knows what the two alternatives represent. Thus one may say that God does not force man. He does not manipulate him like a puppet. On the contrary, he appeals to the high point of his freedom, to choice. But this is a choice of difficult alternatives.

What is Jonah's dilemma? It is simple. Either he can

drag down to death those who are with him (for Jonah knows the wrath of the living God is no jest and God presses his decisions to the very end), or he can admit that he, Jonah, is guilty, accepting the penalty (which is death for him) and committing himself to the will of God. Jonah is free to decide the fate of his companions. He is free to admit his guilt or not. He is free to accept God's will or not. But the alternatives are hard and there is no other option and no compromise. Thus Jonah is summoned once again to accept God's will, i.e., his own condemnation. In thus summoning him God is not playing a game or engaging in a kind of match with man. For what is really at stake? God has revealed to Jonah that Nineveh is under condemnation. He has given him a word to speak to Nineveh which is an intimation but also fundamentally a word of grace, as the end of the story shows. Jonah, however, is not the least bit interested. The condemnation of Nineveh means nothing to him. He has no conception of what it means, and the end of the book will again show how difficult it is to have any such conception. As for carrying God's word, we have already seen about that. But now, by placing Jonah in this dilemma, God seizes him in such a way that Jonah in another form comes up against precisely the thing he did not want to know or do. He did not want to know what was involved in the malediction of Nineveh, and now he himself is under the malediction. God thus makes concrete for him the situation of the other person. So now it is worth considering. Realizing what the condemnation means for him, Jonah can take with full seriousness the condemnation of the other. This will also explain, of course, his stubbornness that it be exacted; he now knows what it involves.

Jonah did not want to carry salvation to Nineveh. But now he is confronted by the same decision. He must carry salvation to the men in the ship. Whether he likes it or not he can no longer escape the signification of his name. He is the "dove" whom the Lord has charged with a message of deliverance. He must fulfill his vocation even aside from the first objective set by God. God catches him, seizes him, and in different forms sets him back in the essential discharge of his vocation.

We have here one of the most remarkable facts in the elucidation of God's action. God respects man's freedom and yet he makes him fulfill in spite of himself the role assigned to him in God's design. We see here the true character of God's patience. It is not inaction. God is not patient in the sense that we are when we wait our turn at the dentist's. His patience is an active power which (in both senses) bears the world, causing it to move to a fixed end, and which also bears each individual, making him advance in the way of God. His patience is also a power which gives the world and each individual enough time for this advance to be their own act, the fruit of their experience, investigation, and choice.

Furthermore, this brings to light in a unique way the responsibility of Jonah, which is that of the Jewish people first, then the Church, and then each of us. For in the last resort Jonah can refuse to admit his guilt. He can continue to outface God and say no. If he does, he knows what the result will be. The vessel will go down with all hands. This is our situation. If in the common danger suspended over the world Christians shun their function, if Christians who have received inestimable grace refuse to take it to the world, then the rest, pagans, non-Christians, those who man the enterprises in which we are engaged, will perish. Christians have to realize that they hold in their hands the fate of their companions in adventure. I weigh these words as I write them. If these companions perish, it will be no injustice, for, after all, they are no better than the rest and they merit their condemnation. The terrible thing is not the injustice; it is the fact that they might have been participants in grace. And if they die in this just condemnation, the responsibility does not rest on them, nor on God, but on Jonah. It is because of Jonah they die. He is wholly responsible for them before God. His situation is not at all a happy one.

The situation is fully explained already in Ezekiel 33.

But if Jonah accepts his condemnation, if the Christian fulfills his proper function in the world, the sailors will be saved. This also means that there is point in all the nautical efforts made to save the vessel. Not for nothing have these various measures been taken. It has given Jonah (and tardy Christians) time to fulfill the word addressed to them, to accept it, and thereby to obtain the indispensable grace. One sees here the value and efficacy of all human means. They are in fact means of postponement until grace comes. They are another aspect of God's patience. And this immense effort of man from the beginning of the ages is a dialogue with this immense grace which is granted to man from the beginning of the ages. But it is essential that none of the partners in the dialogue be missing.

4. THE FIRST PROPHECY

Jonah is the man who accepts his condemnation. He pronounces it himself. He sees that God's will is just in condemning him. "I know it is because of me that this great tempest has come upon you." He justifies God and admits he is right. When the sailors hear this, they begin to cast off their own sin. They lay it on Jonah. Though they do not want to be involved in murder, they also want assurance they are not guilty and they put all their guilt on Jonah. At this point Jonah takes up the role of the scapegoat. And the sacrifice he makes saves them. The sea calms down. He saves them humanly and materially. They will not be drowned because of his fault. He also saves them spiritually before God, for in the eyes of the sailors his accepted sacrifice is such a witness that they are converted.

This summary account brings out clearly the first prophetic aspect of the book. For the one who truly does

36

the things intimated here is not Jonah. In the long run it is of no great weight in itself that Jonah is an example, e.g., of the Christian way. Nor is it of great weight that the sailors were saved. What counts is that this story is in reality the precise intimation of an infinitely vaster story and one which concerns us directly. What Jonah could not do, but his attitude announces, is done by Jesus Christ. He it is who accepts total condemnation. He it is who acknowledges that God is just in condemning him. He it is on whom men lay their sin. He it is by whom men are snatched from death both material and spiritual.

Whether or not the story of Jonah is authentic history does not affect in the least its prophetic character. The important thing is that the story, whether it be biography or inspired fiction, points to Jesus Christ. It is in the light of Jesus Christ that the story is true and Jonah concerns us.

There are, of course, great differences between Jonah and Jesus Christ. Jonah is guilty. Jonah did not want to do God's will. Jonah is not Jesus Christ, just as Joshua and David are not Jesus Christ. But he is one of the long line of types of Jesus, each representing an aspect of what the Son of God will be in totality.

We thus need to point out very carefully the relation between this prophecy and the lessons we have already drawn from the first chapter. The chapter tells us that if it is true that the sacrifice of a man who takes his condemnation can save others around him, then this is far more true when the one sacrificed is the Son of God, God himself. But this analogy must be inverted if we are to get at its full sense. It is not completely true that this acceptance brings about man's salvation *ipso facto*. The balance is not intrinsic. There was nothing that allowed Jonah to say that if he was condemned the storm would abate. We do not have here the propitiatory mechanism which is designed at all costs to appease the will of unknown gods. "At all costs" is the attitude of the sailors. Jonah says: "I know" (v. 12). Jonah counts on the will of God calming the storm. This is not a mechanical effect. It is the reference to a free will that Jonah has learned to know already when he was chosen to carry the word. It is the reference to a good will, and here Jonah is a prophet, for outside Jesus Christ there is no full testimony that God's will is good and his concern is to save man rather than to cause him to perish. It is solely because of the sacrifice of Jesus Christ that the sacrifice of Jonah avails and saves. It is solely because Jesus Christ has accepted malediction that Jonah's acceptance has something to say both to the sailors and to us.

This prophetic aspect of Jonah is stressed yet again by the equally remarkable parallelism between those who put the victim to death. The sailors fear to put a righteous man to death. They call on God to witness that they are no criminals and ask that Jonah's blood should not fall on their heads. In contrast, those who condemn Jesus accept the vengeance of blood: "His blood be on us and on our children" (Matthew 27:25). This difference in attitude expresses the difference there is between Jonah and Jesus, between a man who disobeys God (who is in sin, so that it is no crime to kill him) and the one who has done God's will, so that one can only be a criminal before him, and his blood falls on our heads, the blood which purifies us to all eternity.

And the Lord Appointed a Great Fish

2

And the Lord appointed a great fish to swallow up Jonah; and Jonah was in the belly of the fish three days and three nights. Then Jonah prayed to the Lord his God from the belly of the fish, saying,

"I called to the Lord, out of my distress, and he answered me; out of the belly of Sheol I cried, and thou didst hear my voice. For thou didst cast me into the deep, into the heart of the seas, and the flood was round about me; all thy waves and thy billows passed over me.

Then I said, 'I am cast out from thy presence; how shall I again look upon thy holy temple?' The waters closed in over me, the deep was round about me; weeds were wrapped about my head at the roots of the mountains. I went down to the land whose bars closed upon me for ever; yet thou didst bring up my life from the Pit, O Lord my God.

When my soul fainted within me, I remembered the Lord; and my prayer came to thee, into thy holy temple. Those who pay regard to vain idols forsake their true loyalty. But I with the voice of thanksgiving will sacrifice to thee; what I have vowed I will pay. Deliverance belongs to the Lord."

And the Lord spoke to the fish, and it vomited out Jonah upon the dry land.

If one asks concerning the general theme of this chapter, the point is very clear and simple. The chastised man repents. He comes back to God and God grants pardon and delivers him. But if we stop at this general truth, which is repeated again and again in the historical books of the Bible, we detract a great deal from the relevance and profundity of the text.

1. THE WATERS AND THE FISH

Jonah is thrown into the waters of the raging sea. We should remember the significance of water in the Old Testament and then in the Church. Water denotes swallowing up and death. Yet it is also closely linked with the presence of the Spirit of God. This is part of the general principle that in God's revelation no sign is ever purely negative because God's own action is never negative. Most signs are ambivalent, and that which denotes death also has within it the promise of life. At the beginning of the creation story the waters symbolize the void, nothingness, the abyss. But we cannot stop there: the Spirit of God moves over the face of the waters.

The same applies for those who are in the presence of great masses of water. Thus for Noah in the flood, Moses in the Red Sea, and Joshua in the Jordan, the waters are the power of death and drowning. He who is plunged into them is plunged into death; he who traverses them traverses death. But one cannot traverse them in one's own strength or movement. When a man encounters this force he loses all he is. If he comes out, if he crosses it, it is because God has given him his Spirit, the Holy Spirit, who is linked with the water and who works mysteriously in the work of death. In the presence of the dove, the cloud, and the ark, the Spirit is there to draw back man from destruction and to lead him to life. This man is really dead and he is really brought to life again. A new beginning is offered to him. He is a new creation. We can see the permanent meaning of baptism from the very commencement of revelation.

Jonah is plunged into the waters, and what he tells us in the song shows clearly that this means death. All the terms used are significant. He was "cast into the deep" (v. 3)—a more precise expression than it is with us, denoting a return to primitive chaos, to the void. There is also a reference to the "flood" round about him, and this, too, is a traditional metaphor. In Jewish thought the realm of the dead was surrounded by a river called the Torrent of Destruction. There are several references to this in Scripture, for example, Psalm 18:4; 2 Samuel 22:5. These show that we have once again a specific image charged with meaning.

Again, the strange references to "the roots of the mountains" and the "bars" of the land (v. 6) are not just poetic phrases but bear a specific sense for the Israelites. For Sheol, the realm of the dead, is in fact situated in the mountains and is closed off by a gate with bars (Isaiah 38:10; Job 38:17), and by bolts. Thus Jonah confirms the traditional meaning of water in his song. The saying in verse 4: "I am cast out from thy presence" is a final proof, for the reference here again is to death. For man death is accompanied by dereliction. The man faced with death says: "I am cast out far from thee," and conversely the man who is cast out far from God is in death. Only this man is truly dead. This is unavoidable, for death is simply the visible sign and pain of dereliction, cutting off and separation. Even Jesus Christ in the presence of death had to say: "Why hast thou forsaken me?" Though God is always there, though the dereliction is only apparent, it cannot cease if death is really to be death. Jonah bewails this dereliction. In death he finally comes to see what it means. He who set out to leave God, he who went looking for other gods, he who thought death preferable to obedience—this man now sees what dereliction really is. When it was he who was abandoning God, Jonah accepted it gaily, but now that God has abandoned him he is full of misery. He now knows what death is. He knows that anything is better than being abandoned by God.

* * * * *

But he does not yet know the full measure of his distress. God brings a great fish. It is idle to seek its name or to consider zoological possibilities with a view to identifying the species. It is idle to ask whether the Mediterranean could have contained such a monster. That is not the question. The real question is: Of what is this fish the sign?

For some it is the sign of grace. God deflects death from Jonah when he has him swallowed by a fish. Jonah is alive. He is a prisoner in the belly of the fish, but he is out of danger. This is implicitly the position of all who wish to explain the real presence of the fish as a miracle. This miracle is performed to save Jonah. It is also the position of those who try to explain the story by some natural circumstances, for example, that a ship called "Whale" picked up Jonah. But to argue thus is first to neglect the text. The fish was sent primarily to swallow up, to destroy, to put to death. It was not a means of saving. It confirms the swallowing up by the sea. Again, this view ignores the interpretation which Jesus himself gave and which we ought to study. Finally, to follow this line is to neglect the traditional meaning of the sea-monster in Scripture. The sea-monster, the dragon, or the beast that comes up out of the sea is a well-defined entity in Scripture.

Among the condemnations which the Lord pronounces through the lips of Amos we read: "And though they hide from my sight at the bottom of the sea, there I will command the serpent, and it shall bite them" (9:3). Conversely, among the promises of salvation given to the people, promises which have an eschatological significance, we read: "In that day the Lord with his hard and great and strong sword will punish Leviathan the fleeing serpent, Leviathan the twisting serpent, and he will slay the dragon that is in the sea" (Isaiah 27:1).

There is obviously no point in adducing Leviathan or Behemoth in Job or the beast from the sea in Revelation. Yet these are the same animal; they are the fish that swallowed Jonah.

In every case we have a power of destruction, a power which annihilates, and in so far as this is a symbol we have a power which annihilates spiritually. We are in the presence either of brute force unleashed or of the force of evil, the evil one himself. This is not to say the monster is Satan. Not at all! The monster does not have the same role, but it is an unleashed and aggressive force of the evil one. We also know that this unleashed force is obliged to obey when God commands, for example, when it is a matter of destroying those whom God wishes to punish. This is how it is with Jonah. God in using this force uses it in its own terms. He uses it to destroy. We should know, too, that God will finally destroy this power, since it has no more place in the new creation. The intervention of the great fish, then, is not at all a sign of grace, of Jonah delivered from the waters. On the contrary, it is the climax of the condemnation, the seal on the act of death, the presence of what is beyond remedy. It is damnation. The fish is in fact hell. Jonah has thus traversed the agony and death and come to this hell prepared by God to enforce the total separation of man and God.

I do not think this is a subjective view of hell like that of the hell in our lives. On the contrary, hell here is in very truth the objective place of the total solitude of the condemned man who in death finds the cutting off of all ties, the closing of all hope, a world just as radically restricted as the belly of the fish in the bosom of the tempest. No more help is possible and God is in heaven.

This is no mere feeling (I felt I was in hell, said Rimbaud). It is no relative experience (a veritable hell, said Von Paulus of Stalingrad, and the fact that he used "veritable" shows that it was not really hell). What Jonah encounters is absolute hell.

What Jonah finds is also what he sought when he looked for a place where God would not be. And one might show the irony of this kind of answer, which we can sometimes get too. Jonah really wanted to go where he would be separated from God and would no longer hear his word. He is now there, in hell, but it is not where he wanted to go. Yet it is the only place corresponding to his wish. Not totally so, for this hell, like the fish, serves God's word. God is still the master there. But this does not alter the fact that for Jonah the separation is total. His prayer, however, will bring about his liberation.

All this shows yet again that the chief aim of the story is not to give historical information, even though the miracle of the fish is quite acceptable, and I for my part see no objection to the possibility of a miracle of this kind. It is obvious that God's power can manifest itself thus. The main point to consider, however, is what this miracle really signifies. If the facts recorded are just facts, if they just happened historically, then Jonah did not really go down to death or enter hell. This means that we cannot take with full seriousness what he says in the psalm. He is exaggerating; it is hyperbole, oriental exaggeration, poetic imagination. We cannot regard these words as an expression of truth but only as a frenzied song. They are indeed false. For Jonah finally says: "I went down. . . ." He is stating facts. On this view, however, the facts are not in keeping with the reality. We have to interpret: "I nearly. . . ." But if we take it thus, if Jonah did no more than almost die, if he was simply in great fear, but then the fish came along to save him from death, the story no longer makes any real sense. It ceases to be prophetic. Jonah's story is no longer of interest to us. What lesson can we draw from it? That of the divine omnipotence which creates the monster at the right moment? But we must admit that this is weak and contrary to the ongoing revelation which reaches its goal in Jesus Christ. To keep a miracle which no longer has any true point, we destroy the revelation in the text.

I think we take the text much more seriously if we put the waters and the fish among the biblical symbols for death and hell. We must also believe the text when it tells us that Jonah really faced death, that he died, that he went down into hell. The moment we do this the story takes on exemplary significance. It is of value to all of us. For if there is little risk of the adventure of Jonah befalling us, death awaits us all. Thus the text acquires the very high value it is accorded by the traditions and by Jesus Christ, as we shall see. Nevertheless there is no doubt but that we must be very cautious in making such statements, since they are not true for all the books of the Bible or for all the stories. They become true only when they are in agreement with the rest of the biblical revelation without changing its direction. In no sense are we to interpret the symbols by secret keys, traditions, etc. We are to interpret them solely by the Bible itself. The consensus of the records of the ongoing thought which is revelation allows us to seize on what may be symbolical elements in it, but always with the realization that we must keep as much as possible to facts as facts, since revelation has always to be incarnate. Hence, there can be no single method of interpretation. As the different books fall into different categories, so there must be many different categories of interpretation, though always related to the unvarying central line: Jesus Christ.

2. THE SONG OF JONAH

Exegetes have treated the psalm in the second chapter with great severity. They do not think it can be an original or authentic part of the story. Linguistic arguments are advanced into which it would be useless to go, but which are most uncertain in view of modern researches which have shaken classical ideas of the development of Hebrew. We may leave all this on one side without loss. The great argument against the validity of the psalm, however, is that it is not a psalm of appeal and petition, but an act of thanksgiving and praise. Jonah is in the fish, but though his position can hardly be comfortable he does not ask to be let free. If we take the story realistically, he does not have long to live in the belly of the fish; and if we get at the heart of the meaning, he is in hell and hence in the worst of all possible situations. Yet in his address to God he does not ask that God should either liberate him or pardon him. He praises him for deliverance, because he is saved, because he is reconciled with God, because he has found God's grace again. At a first glance this seems to be both impossible and incomprehensible. Thus a simple solution has been put forward. At first the story of Jonah contained only the facts. Jonah was swallowed by the fish and then at God's command vomited up on the shore, with nothing between. Then a copyist or commentator, seeking to explain God's decision, found a psalm which seemed fairly close to Jonah's adventure, and by way of explanation he inserted it at the place where we know it today.

As I see it, this interpretation runs up against two serious objections. The first is that if we take away the song we break the relation between man and God which the story emphasizes so strongly. This part becomes a kind of absurd demonstration of the divine arbitrariness. If it is alleged that a commentator felt constrained to alter the text, it is hard to see why he should replace some previous explanation by this psalm. This is all highly improbable.

The second objection is even more serious. As usual, the historian who dreamed up this view seems to have regarded the commentators who amended the text as imbeciles. Why did they choose a text which fitted so badly? Why did they not emend and adapt it? In particular, why did they not change the tenses and cut out the statements that God has already saved Jonah? If the commentators simply inserted the text without adapting it, this was stupid, and when one is acquainted with the patience, competence, erudition and acuteness of the rabbis in the centuries before Christ, it is perfectly ridiculous to suppose them capable of such oversights and blunderings. Furthermore, if we believe the redactor was capable of these, why not the author of the book too? This is just as likely. In fact, it is best to abandon this hypothesis and to take the text as a whole. It also seems to be impermissible to speak of such alterations if one can explain the text in some other way. It is best to begin with the idea that the text is authentic and to try to get at its deep meaning.

Now is there any explanation of the song on our view? Can we solve the problem it poses by some inner necessity or profound meaning? To my mind this can be done quite easily. Jonah, even while he is not saved, even while he is at the nadir of his misery, in hell, suddenly rediscovers the permanence of grace: "I called to the Lord, out of my distress, and he answered me." Jonah has not been answered if we take the answer to be rescue from the belly of the fish, salvation from hell. But he has been answered if we take the answer to be adoption under the care of the God who takes on the totality of our sufferings, dramas and situations. He is answered because grace does not fail in any way, and even if there is no visible, actual and personal sign, Jonah can state that the answer takes place because grace has been granted to him from all eternity. Jonah rediscovers this grace of God at the very moment his situation is hopeless and to all appearances nothing more is to be expected. His refusal and flight were clearly outside grace. Events have taken place without any indication of a favorable intervention, only signs of judgment. But suddenly, when he has accepted his condemnation, when he has acknowledged before God that he was guilty and that

48

God was just, he sees that at no point did God cease to show him grace. Under condemnation in hell he finds the faithfulness which permits him to say: "Thou hast answered me." In his return to God he comes to know God again. There is no bargain: "I repent and so you show grace." God has been gracious from the very beginning. He does not change when man returns to him. He simply brings to light his hidden mercy and makes his general and eternal benediction near and actual. In all these twists, in this debate, in the fall of Jonah, grace has never left him. Quite the contrary! But it is in hell that he really comes to take account of it.

The song also shows that this grace is eternal as well as permanent. Grace was not shown him only when the word came to him. He was the object of grace from all eternity, before the circumstances of his life unfolded, before he had any choice to obey or to refuse, before he ever lent an ear to this divine word, before he learned his membership in the people of God or the law which is God's will, before his eyes opened and his lips cried, before all the reality of his human life. From all eternity he was an object of this grace which he now perceives as light in the belly of the fish, as living reality enclosed in hell.

Nothing proves this to Jonah. No fact confirms his insight. He does not have even the first beginning of deliverance. But simply in the very fact that he has been able to repent, to condemn himself, to recognize the sentence of the just judge, he has reason enough to say: "Thou hast delivered me." It is here indeed that the great decision is taken. After falling the natural man can say only: "It is not my fault, it is the fault of others, and it is God's fault." Adam and Eve say this in each of us as they did in Genesis. The moment when I say: "It is my fault," is the moment the lancet of grace has pierced the abscess and drained the situation for which there was no outlet.

Now one must certainly differentiate this accusation from the unhealthy mania of self-accusation and masochism. It is not on a sick man that grace brings about this change. It is a sane, rough, stable, and combative man that it brings to the foot of the cross. Sick self-accusation is a satanic counterfeit of the work of grace. Either way it takes the power of the Holy Spirit or that of Satan to change human nature and bring man to humiliation and repentance. It is this change which allows Jonah to see the action of grace. Alone he could not have said on the ship what he did say. But God acts in his heart and brings about the terrible conversion which Jonah recognizes as such. Subsequently, God does not spare the man who has been converted from trials, condemnation, and death. Those whom God pursues thus are not privileged by human reckoning. But whatever comes they know they can build on the grace which has brought about their conversion (in the strong sense of turning again).

It is this turning again which allows Jonah to say he has already been heard, his salvation is already a reality. At the bottom of hell he no longer doubts but that he will see the temple of the Lord. He thus gives thanks, and in truth one can do no other after grasping the persistence of God's love. Hence it is quite understandable that this should be a psalm of thanksgiving and not of petition. What more is there to ask? Other things are small compared with this great decision of God to stay by Jonah. "If God is for us, who is against us?" Jonah has still to be delivered from the fish, but this is no longer what matters in the first instance. It is also understandable that Jonah should speak in the past tense, for he has laid hold of this past act of God which is enough, and since he leans on this God who is present in his love, he leans on an action which he can be sure will be brought to a successful conclusion now it has begun. "God's word shall not return to him empty. . . ."

A final fact confirms this interpretation. Jonah has understood the permanence and eternity of God's love. And when he obeys and goes to condemn Nineveh he cherishes this thought; this explains his reaction to God when he sees that God will not destroy Nineveh. He knew all along—he had lived it out—that God does not abandon the sinner.

For the difficulties raised by the psalm there is thus an explanation which is sufficiently simple, and which is in accord both with the biblical revelation as a whole and also with the text of Jonah. This permits us to dispense with exegetical theories which are advanced in precisely the same measure as there is failure to understand the text.

* * * * *

This agony of Jonah is in fact the agony of every man. Jonah does not undergo an adventure which is exceptional. Jonah in the sea and Jonah in the fish—this is the situation of each of us in the crisis of life and not just the final conflict with death. For there is no very great difference between the man who is spiritually dead because he wants to be separated from God and the man who is engulfed in the raging sea.

Every man lives above the abyss. Like Jonah on the waves, he lives over the twofold abyss of perdition and death. The abyss, Scripture teaches, is not just a bottomless hole. It is an active power which seeks to take possession and destroy the creation of God. There is good reason for personifying death. Death is not a kind of lottery governed by the law of numbers and turning up as heart failure. It is a force which comes, which addresses each of us personally, which progressively cuts into life, which wears and wastes it away, which breaks it up and corrodes it with satanic skill, until the day comes when there is nothing left. We are in constant relation with our death. When we try to cling fast to time, we are battling this force from the abyss as Jonah perhaps tried to swim in the storm. In the same way the abyss plunges us into daily temptation, lays for us a fatal snare, provokes us to doubt the word of God and the grace of God which might have been shown us, and destroys every moment the conviction that God creates in us. This double aggression drives us to hell.

Only at moments do we confront the abyss and recognize it for what it is. It is the crisis of life at any moment. It is the destruction in an instant of a pious and saintly life. It is the agony of a man's life. It may sometimes, too, be a salutary crisis which comes with the defeat of the abyss when its jaw closes with a crunching of teeth which meet only the void: man saved by grace, man awakened to new life.

If I recall these well-known facts, it is because the psalm of Jonah gives us teaching which accords with revelation as a whole. To return to the text, we see that everything relating to the abyss is in the past tense: "the flood was round about me. . . . the deep was round about me. . . . the bars closed upon me for ever." Nevertheless, as we have seen, Jonah is not yet saved. He is in the worst possible situation, in hell. The power of the abyss does not seem to have been weakened for him. On the other hand, the divine action described in the song is at one and the same time both past and future: "Thou answered me . . . thou didst hear my voice. . . . thou didst bring up my life. . . . I will sacrifice to thee . . . I will pay. . . . deliverance belongs to the Lord."

This kind of affirmation is very common in the Bible. When one speaks of the work of death, Satan, and the abyss, one speaks in the past. In contrast, when one speaks of God's work one speaks in the future. But this is only in translation. To get the real contrast, it must be remembered that there are only two tenses in Hebrew grammar, the perfect and the imperfect. The perfect signifies a completed and terminated action which does not go on and has no further developments. The imperfect denotes a continuing action which was begun earlier, still goes on, and will extend into the future in a way and to a time not yet determined. The saying about Christ that he was, he is,

52

and he comes can all be rendered in Hebrew by a single tense which expresses this permanence.

We may thus say rather more precisely that in most cases the work of the abyss is in the perfect in the Bible, while that of God is in the imperfect. What does this very instructive verbal form mean, then, for Jonah and for us? First, it means that the action of the abyss is ended. It exists, we see it with distinct reality, we are in the midst of it as Jonah was in the sea. It seems there is no common denominator between the reality of this action and the terribly unreal grace of God. Mortal aggression is concretely in evidence for each of us. It is also beyond remedy. Since it is past, we cannot change it. It is the first fall, original sin. It took place once for us all. In spite of our good intentions and desires, in spite of our intelligence and virtue, we cannot modify this finished work, the work of the fall and the work of death, which ineluctably reproduces itself in all of us because it has come to all of us with all its force and we are dependent on this past which we absolutely cannot change.

At the same time, another aspect of this past should also be stressed. The work of death is done. It has no future. Man cannot question it, no doubt, but it is terminated. It has already reached its term and climax. It cannot develop any more. It cannot do anything new. Neither Satan, abyss, nor death is really active any more. We suffer the consequences, but nothing new can come in this domain. It is perpetually the same history which begins afresh with each of us. It can go no further. The abyss has reached the limits it cannot pass. It has its weapons and cannot forge any new ones. It has its power and cannot develop it further. It has its victims and cannot augment their number. It draws all its resources from what has been, and its force is thus limited.

In contrast, the describing of God's work in the imperfect implies that this work, having begun, continues, develops, and rests on continually new initiatives on God's

53

part. The work of God has a future before it. It is not a completed and abandoned work. It is not a risk the Creator took. It is a majestic adventure which moves on to its consummation by ways which are constantly renewed by God's love. All the future belongs to the Lord. He does not share it with anyone else. This is why we find that there can be no conflict between the abyss and the Lord. The Lord infinitely surpasses the abyss. He could crush it by a word if he wanted. There is no conflict, and God is never endangered by the demon as in most cosmogonies. Hell, like everything else, obeys God.

This means for man that if Satan's work is a reality into which he is plunged, the Lord's work is the object of faith and hope, begun but not yet visible, moving to its consummation and perfection. Man's situation above the abyss is not a final one. It is not one of maximum danger. All that we can fear from the abyss has been achieved already. We know it. To be sure, the danger is formidable enough. But it is not beyond a solution or hopeless. It is limited. The teeth of the beast are blunted. It is held on a chain. We know for certain that the work which lifts man out of Sheol will really be completed. Its main development is ahead. The greatest miracles are only a small beginning.

This is what is implied by the contrast of tenses in the song of Jonah and in the rest of Scripture too.

* * * * *

Jonah, when he cries and thanks God, is in the depths of hell. He has passed into death. He is rejected, condemned. Yet he still speaks to God and God hears his prayer. God will bring him out of this situation from which there is no exit. One must not deduce from this that the situation of the dead may change, that they can continue to do meritorious works, that prayers can modify their lot, and that there is a kind of purgatory. Jonah is not in purgatory; he is in hell. Any other interpretation is rejected and negated by other texts, so that there is no need to pursue the matter. But the story adds another certainty which we can hear only if we remember that this is a prophetic text.

Jonah saw again that he was bound to God the moment he accepted his condemnation, confessed to the sailors this great and mighty God who does all that he wills to do, and submitted to his judgment. At this moment he was with God. He "remembered the Lord" (v. 7) in this great danger, and God responded. Hence, when Jonah was plunged into death and hell, he was not separated from God. Nothing can put a barrier between us and our Savior once a little movement on our part has restored this link which God patiently re-establishes for us. God is with Jonah in the depths of the ocean. God is with Jonah in the belly of the fish. God is with each of us in death. When human bonds are snapped, when coma arrests human actions, when there is agony, the invisible and decisive debate, behind the petrified mask, we can know that this is both a last trial (that which Jesus knew, apparent abandonment between the pale hands of nothingness) and also a final dialogue with the Savior. Hell does not merely obey this almighty Lord; it is also open to him. As we enter it, God also enters it so as not to leave us alone. This is why Jesus himself was in the realm of the dead; this is why he descended into hell. Jesus knew the same agony, the same dereliction; the gates of hell are open to him, and, as Dante said, the most secret wall of the strongest town in hell has crumbled to let God's envoy pass. Thus the breach is made. Hell is no longer closed. It is no longer the stronghold where Satan guards his triumphs. Hell is robbed of its certainties.

If Jonah can address God thus from the inside of the monster—a rare thing in the Old Testament—it is because he announces as a prophet that Jesus himself has come where he is. Jesus does not abandon those who have been given him by his Father. He goes to look for them where they are, in the depths of their condemnation.

55

All that we say about Jonah, which is true for each of us, is also true for the Church when it holds debate in the midst of perils and sees itself plunged into death, into the heart of the world.

But Jonah's psalm to God suggests another thought. "When my soul fainted within me, I remembered the Lord," says Jonah. It was precisely in the presence of death, in the dramatic dilemma sketched earlier, that he remembered the Lord. And God replies. He answers the cry of man in need. Some try to explain the later fluctuations in Jonah (chapters 3 and 4) by saying that his conversion was not a real one, that it was only external, because it was the result of his distress. We shall see that this explains nothing. But it is a widespread idea that prayer in time of danger and conversion as a result of sufferings *in extremis* are of no worth. Once again man is far more inflexible and rigorous in his judgments than God. There are no grounds at all for scorning Jonah's conversion *in extremis*. Quite the contrary, for God takes it seriously. God always takes seriously the cry of man in distress, of suffering man, of man face to face with death. What, perhaps, he does not take so seriously is the cold, calculated, rational decision of the man who weighs the odds and condescendingly accepts the hypothesis of God.

That the conversion which God accepts is an interested one is self-evident. Every conversion is interested. Who can dare to say that his own life and death are of no concern to him? What ridiculous idealism would make us so pure, so spiritual, so objective that we could be converted for any other reason than because we were in danger of death and dangers of all kinds? To claim for oneself an abstract and idealistic conversion of this kind is to pretend to bring to God a valuable sacrifice, a perfect man. It is to want to replace Christ. It is to reach the summit of arrogance. The cry which God hears comes from the depths of the abyss, from sickness and suffering, from the heart which is humbled, bruised, and despairing. This is the cry which produces conversion because things cannot stay as they are, and conversion is a change of route for man. The moment a man decides to change his style of life in this way, the moment he remembers God again, his way which was plunging more and more deeply into the dark is suddenly directed to the light in a dizzy reascent. The truth is that God responds, not to our better feelings, but to the desperate cry of the man who has no other help but God. God responds just because man is in trouble and has nowhere to turn.

Obviously, when man has somewhere to turn he does not pray to God and God does not come to him. As long as man can invent hopes and methods, he naturally suffers from the pretension that he can solve his own problem. He invents technical instruments, the state, society, money, and science. He also invents idols, magic, philosophy, spiritualism, and all these things give him hope in himself that he can direct his own life and control his destiny. They all cause him to turn his back on God. As long as there is a glimmer of confidence in these means man prefers to stake his life on them rather than handing it over to God. When the sailors tried to save the ship by their nautical skill, Jonah slept. All these aids had to be shattered, all solutions blocked, and man's possibilities hopelessly outclassed by the power of the challenge, to cause Jonah to return to God. Only when man has lost the vast apparatus of civilization, in personal response, does man remember God.

When man relies on these instruments: "those who pay regard to vain idols" (v. 8); when he stakes his life on the state or money, he does not know personal mercy. For these idols which help him to live are without mercy. They can indeed give a great deal to man. They can solve his problems. They can grant him happiness, power, even virtue and good. But they cannot give him the very thing he needs, mercy. For these idols have no heart. No relation of love can be set up with them, only relations of possession. If the one loves, the other possesses. The man who loves money or the state is not loved by them; he is owned. This is why so many fundamental problems of man cannot be solved by these powers. For man has definitive need only of one thing, to be loved, which also means to be pardoned and lifted above himself. None of these idols (least of all eros love) can do this for him. But man does not know this, or hear it, until he has learned the emptiness of idols, until he has been disillusioned, until in truth he finds himself naked and without mercy, until he begs in an empty world for the mercy which cannot come to him from the world. To this stripped man God responds as he does to Jonah, and Jonah learns where mercy is to be had, and who can give it to him, and he gets it because for once in his life he turns to the one who is in fact merciful.

3. THE SECOND PROPHECY

The second chapter is singularly rich in prophetic content. We again recall that all we have said above is true only to the degree that it is a prophecy of Jesus Christ. Furthermore, it is chiefly in this chapter that what we have said is confirmed, namely, that in this book the situation in which Jonah is placed rather than the person of Jonah is the real matter of the prophecy and that which sends us back to Jesus Christ.

The prophecy has here several aspects; we shall deal with the first elements very briefly.

First, if Jonah is thrust into the abyss, it is because he separates himself from God. He had adopted the attitude of man without God, and it is to this degree that he knows the totality of dereliction. But in this respect he is also a witness and prophet of the one who, being God, was without God in order to be with us. He is also a prophet of the humiliation of Jesus, who sets aside his superiority in order to descend into the abyss of men, and of the dereliction of Jesus on the cross to go even into hell. What is intimated is not just that if Jonah can still pray to God it is because Jesus has already subjected the power of hell to his Father. What is really intimated is the adventure of Jesus. What happens to Jonah happens to Jesus. For Jesus took on him the fulness of man.

We are thus confronted here by the insoluble mystery of the unity of all men in Christ. If all are dead in Adam, all are made alive in Christ. This is why the Book of Jonah, so rich in instruction for each of us (our life, our personal problems), for Israel, and for the Church, is also the prophetic book of Jesus Christ. Jesus truly lives the life of each of us. All that Jonah is in his abandonment, revolt, and misery, and later in his discussions with God, all this Christ has assumed, transformed into prophecy who the Savior and Messiah is and what he will do. Conversely, it is also a revelation that what happens to Christ will all happen to man. If Christ in Jesus takes on our adventures and condition, he gives us in exchange his own sanctity and righteousness. The Book of Jonah is essentially prophetic of this twofold relation.

But to say that it is prophetic is to say not only that it is inspired by the Holy Spirit but also that what it signifies is the action of the Holy Spirit. For what we have just said about the relation between Christ and each of us denoted in this book implies the presence of the Holy Spirit, since it is through him that we receive the communication of the righteousness of God in Jesus Christ—and it is this that we recognize in the psalm from the depths of hell.

* * * * *

But the most important element is obviously the express declaration in which Jesus refers this adventure to himself. When the Pharisees ask Jesus for a sign he answers: " 'An evil and adulterous generation seeks for a sign; but no sign shall be given to it except the sign of the prophet Jonah. For as Jonah was three days and three nights in the belly of the whale, so will the Son of man be three days and three nights in the heart of the earth. The men of Nineveh will arise at the judgment with this generation and condemn it; for they repented at the preaching of Jonah, and behold, something greater than Jonah is here'" (Matthew 12:39-41). The reply is repeated more briefly by Matthew when Jesus is asked for a sign from heaven (16:4). Finally, Luke has it with a slight difference of sense: "When the crowds were increasing, he began to say, 'This generation is an evil generation; it seeks a sign, but no sign shall be given to it except the sign of Jonah. For as Jonah became a sign to the men of Nineveh, so will the Son of man be to this generation. . . . The men of Nineveh will arise at the judgment . . . for they . . .'" (11:29-32). In the Lucan passage the reference to the miracle is less precise and the conversion of the Ninevites is related to it directly, whereas Matthew does not do this but speaks of Jonah's preaching. Nevertheless, the three days and nights in the belly of the fish are clearly implied in Luke's Gospel too.

These sayings of Jesus pose two questions. The one concerns the prophetic significance which Jesus ascribes to the adventure of Jonah; the other concerns the true meaning of the sayings themselves, which is not so obvious as it might seem.

As concerns the prophetic character of Jonah, the problem is simple enough. When Jesus refers to the sign that Jonah was three days and nights in the belly of the fish, and says that no other sign will be given, or when in a fuller version he establishes the comparison with the Son of man who will rest three days and nights in the heart of the earth, he has in view his death, burial, and resurrection. This confirms our interpretation of Jonah's fish. God brings Jesus out of the depths of hell as he brought Jonah. Jesus Christ wholly fulfills all prophecies, all that the Holy Spirit intimated in advance in order that Yahweh's power, love, and constancy might be evident to us. Moreover, the text of the psalm spoken by Jonah allows us to be a little more precise. In his agony Jonah tells us that his soul fainted but his prayer rose up to God, and this recalls Gethsemane, just as verse 4 recalls the dereliction on the cross and verse 6 the descent into hell. In all this Jesus Christ confirms and attests that these words are inspired by his Father, and he shows that Scripture carries salvation because he has accomplished it.

The text thus receives both a consecration and also a singular dignity, for it is the only one to announce clearly, to predict, what will happen to the Son of God. Hence we cannot place it among the pious stories of the Haggadah. It receives this dignity *a posteriori* through the sayings and death of Jesus Christ (as do most of the other Old Testament texts, but to a higher degree). The remarkable thing, however, is that even when there was nothing to suggest that it should be taken seriously, it was set apart in the 6th century B.C. by the Jews, who differentiated it from other works of the same type. This was with a view to and in some way in expectation of this unforeseeable consecration by Jesus Christ.

* * * * *

But we must also investigate the meaning of this saying of Jesus. He tells us that the sign of Jonah ought to suffice for this perverse generation. It will get no other sign apart from this. Jesus refuses to give a sign to the Jews in self-demonstration. Why? Before we answer this question a preliminary question arises. If the sign of Jonah did not really take place, of what value is the saying of Jesus? When Jesus recalls the sign he seems to regard it as historical. Is not this reference enough to close the discussion and to force us humbly to accept that the miracle took place?—our task being simply to adore and to believe, not to discuss and explain. I must admit that this does not satisfy me. This attitude seems to smack more of sloth than humility, and it is not at all to God's glory, since it fails to divide the Scriptures.

The statement of Jesus does not have to have this implication. Jesus as true man had no special information on scientific matters. His eyes did not see ultra-violet rays nor did his ears hear sub-sonic sounds. But his eyes saw the heart of man and his ears heard the words of God and his mind pondered the Scriptures. The point is that Jesus had a divine nature in relation to truth, but not in relation to the material or immaterial reality of creation. Thus he might well have been content with the ideas of contemporary Jews concerning the miracle of Jonah. Jesus was not interested in historical criticism or scientific exegesis (which ought to put historians and exegetes in their very lowly place); nor is this the important thing. But Jesus made no mistake concerning the spiritual meaning and prophetic character of the story of Jonah. His teaching relates to the truth in it, not to the historicity of the miracle. Whether the miracle took place or not is not the thing that counts; what counts is that it is recorded in a book which was accepted as revelation because of its spiritual meaning. What counts is that it is declared to us as God's word. God's word in the story has value, not the miracle as such. We know that the devil can work miracles. Pharaoh's magicians did many of the things Moses did. The difference is that this miracle is attested both as God's word and by God's word. This gives the true thrust and worth to the miracle and not *vice versa.*

When we make the question of reality the central one we miss the point that what we are to believe is not the miracle but the word of God. The miracle has nothing of its own to give. What is really true is the word of God.

Thus the question put to each of us is much more serious than whether we think God has the power to do this miracle. It is whether we find in the Book of Jonah a word of God which concerns us. This means on the one side that we should see our resemblance to Jonah, and that we cannot make ourselves better than we are even in virtue of our election. Above all, it means on the other side that we are to believe in what it declares, in the life which is promised to us because of the resurrection of Jesus Christ.

62

We have to believe in God's word rather than the miracle. It is quite possible to believe in the miracle without being committed at all, just as it is possible to believe the newspapers when they say someone has broken the sound barrier. This kind of belief remains outside me, and if God only had revelations of this kind to convey to man, he could not have assured the salvation of anyone. If, however, the real problem is that of God's word in Jonah, my own life is involved and I can no longer regard the story as mere history but as the story of my relations with God in Jesus Christ. The real question is not just that of the miracle done for Jonah; it is that of the miracle done for me. The real question is not that of the fish which swallowed Jonah; it is that of the hell where I am going and already am. The real question is not that of the strange obedience of the fish to God's command; it is that of the resurrection of Jesus Christ and my resurrection. This is not so through tendentious wresting of the text. It is so because the text does not mean anything else and was not written for any other purpose.

One thus sees why it is so important not to be so worried about the material side of the miracle. If the real issue is my own death and resurrection, I cannot build on the story of the fish. My salvation and resurrection do not depend on the resurrection of Jonah. The miracle of Jonah does not guarantee me anything. It is on God's word which records the miracle that my salvation rests. It is because God declares it to me that it comes about. He also declares it to me in the story of Jonah. This is the truth of the story. It is true because it is a word of God, not because it corresponds to historical reality.

Yet if it does not record historical facts, we are tempted to say that the Bible deceives us or lies. How then can we have confidence in it? How could Jesus build on a misleading text? We must remember, however, that this is a prophetic text, a divine word which intimates what will be in Christ, not what will be in human history (prediction) nor what has been (history). The measure of the reality of prophecy is fulfilment, and this is precisely what we see. The miracle of Jonah becomes true and actual in and by the miracle of the resurrection of Jesus Christ. It does not have its value or reality in itself. It is prophecy. It becomes true in its fulfilment. This is why Jesus can build on the text. He knows his own death will authenticate it. This is why the text is no lie whether or not the story actually took place. But this means that the adventure of Jonah is that of Jesus. We are thus led to put the second question.

What does Jesus mean precisely by his answer: "No sign shall be given to it except the sign of Jonah"? Man was seeking signs; he always does. His attitude is always that if God will work some miracle he, man, will believe. But the miracles God does perform are never enough. When Jesus answers the Pharisees he has already worked miracles. He has cleansed the leper, healed the paralytic, raised the daughter of Jairus. But this does not count in their eyes. A past miracle no longer has any value. There must always be something new. Things go awry and man demands that God put them straight. There are wars and famines, and man demands that God alter the order of the world. He demands the miracle for the sake of the miracle, for himself, and strictly as a proof of God. But it will never be an adequate proof. We have here a dramatic misunderstanding. The miracle God performs is not a proof but an attestation of his love. It is not a restoration of order, a due which man can exact, but an act of grace in which God comes to man. Now when man asks for miracles he does not in the least ask for God's presence. The only vital miracle (God with us) is not man's wish. "An evil and adulterous generation seeks for a sign. . . ." It is evil and adulterous just because it seeks for a sign. To demand a sign as it does is to show that it is far from God, estranged from grace and divorced from his love. If it were not, it would not seek a sign but God himself. In face of this dreadful misunderstanding, Jesus refuses a sign. It would be useless to give one, since this would simply confirm the generation in its adultery instead of converting it. The men of our day, avid for technical and social miracles, demand miracles from the Church in its own sphere. The Church should not accede to this request. The sign of Jonah should suffice for our generation as it did for that of Jesus' day.

The sign of Jonah should suffice. This extraordinary reference to a past miracle implies first that it is *the* miracle, and then that if this does not suffice nothing will convince us. The prophetic history of Jonah is *the* miracle. It is the only true miracle, for in effect it is that of the resurrection of Jesus Christ. Here we have the fulness of God's love, not for one man but for all, not for a moment but for eternity. All miracles are simply feeble lights like beacons on our way to the port where shines the light, the total light of the resurrection. All miracles finally refer to this one and find their explanation in it. It is *the* miracle.

It is, however, the very one which men do not seek and which they do not expect: the presence of Christ. But what do other miracles signify without this? What would be signified by the raising of Jairus' daughter for a brief span if at the end of her life she would simply fall back forever into the same dark pit? What would the restoration of the leper's health mean if it was simply so that he could use his life as we all do in evil and perdition, to rediscover sickness and old age and at the last the abyss? All this means nothing. All our organizations and techniques and works and churches and miracles are meaningless if they take place with the same limitation, if we do not have God with us. This is why Jonah is in truth *the* miracle. To the degree that he shows God staying with man in death and hell (all forms of hell, including those we know on earth), to the degree that the miracle of Jonah is that of Christ's resurrection, we really need no other miracle. This is a true miracle.

The remarkable thing, however, is that Jesus does not refer to his own resurrection; he refers to the miracle of Jonah. This is a striking lesson. He does not say: "Wait a bit, you will see me rise again." He says: "There is the sign of Jonah; if you do not believe that, the rest is useless." It is true that if we do not believe the word of God in the Book of Jonah we will not believe the rest. The resurrection of Jesus has no definitive power to convince. Some have tried to conceal it for political reasons. Some have thrown doubt on the credibility of the witnesses. Some have invoked scientific reasons and historical criticism. Some have given rational explanations. Some accept it as a good pious tradition. Some see in it a myth. The resurrection of Jesus is no more convincing than the story of Jonah, and our hard hearts do not accept it any more easily. Even if we had been there the fact alone would not have been enough to persuade us. The soldiers and the members of the Sanhedrin were not convinced. What convinced the disciples was the work of the Holy Spirit. When Jesus makes this reply, then, he refers his questioners to the decisive thing of which we have spoken, the authority of God's word. "Do you see in the miracle of Jonah a word of God which has come to you? If so, you need no other sign, for by the Holy Spirit you see in this one, which is prophetic, a word of God, and you believe it will be fulfilled. If not, no other sign will convince you; other signs are useless and will only confirm you in your unbelief."

This is the point of the answer. It is still true for us. For the resurrection of Jesus is attested to us by the same word and lit up by the same Holy Spirit as the story of Jonah. We have no other proof or certitude. We are asked to believe this word which affirms it to us and to accept the same Spirit who convinces us. The resurrection of Jesus intimated by the Book of Jonah is thus enlightened in this twofold way, by the twofold action of the Holy Spirit. Before it took place it was announced from the depths of the centuries. A ray of light comes from the night to strike this point in history which is the empty tomb. It is the prophecy of Jonah, which is true because it announces this true thing. Now that it has taken place, it is confirmed in the inner heart of every man elected by God. A ray of light comes from the heart to lead to this point of his history which is the empty tomb. In both cases, both before and after, it is the Holy Spirit who works, objectively on the one side and subjectively on the other. In both cases we know from whom the truth comes and on whom it focuses.

What Jesus means, then, is that it is not the material fact which suffices or which signifies anything. It is the word of God which makes the sign both clear and certain. In his mercy God gives all that is needed to accept his word spoken in the Book of Jonah. Even before Jesus came it was possible to believe this word, to accept it for what it is. This was asked of the Jews. But after the resurrection of Jesus Christ, we know why this word was spoken and we take it more seriously by referring it to the sole miracle, Jesus Christ living eternally for us.

Thus the whole adventure of Jonah, now that Jesus Christ has come, has no more meaning at all if we seek to give it a different sense.

* * * * *

A final word has still to be spoken. Jonah, as we have often said, is a prophecy of Jesus Christ and also our own story. This narrative expresses both a reality of man and also a reality of God's action. Without undue wresting we can thus see in the swallowing up of Jonah a sign of baptism. It is not just the fact of the water, though attention should be paid to the spiritual meaning of water, as we have shown. It is more precisely the significance which the drowning of Jonah has in the story, that of spiritual disappearance, of entry into the abyss, and of a return from it. Now this is just what baptism represents along with union with Christ, which is implied by the story even though not explicit. There can be no doubt, too, that the resurrection is in view, as we have seen, and this also points to the new birth. When he comes forth from the fish Jonah is a new man, a new creature, like the one who has passed through baptism, at least in the reality of this baptism.

From the various angles from which we consider the story, then, we find this relation to baptism. And while this is not of major or decisive importance, it does at least throw light on the fact that baptism means intimate and complete union with the risen Lord. It is in this sense that baptism is integration into the Church, not as an organization, but as the body of Christ. As Jonah is in the story a baptized man, prophetically set in the precise situation of Christ, so the baptized person is united with Christ, not just prophetically now, but because he reproduces the death and resurrection in this act, and thereby participates in the body of Christ which is on earth and whose head is in heaven. The two adventures, that of Jonah and that of the baptized, both have truth only to the degree that it is the Holy Spirit who makes them participant in and contemporary with the adventure, the life, of Jesus Christ himself.

Then the Word of the Lord Came to Jonah a Sec- ond Time

3

Then the word of the Lord came to Jonah the second time, saying, "Arise, go to Nineveh, that great city, and proclaim to it the message that I tell you." So Jonah arose and went to Nineveh, according to the word of the Lord. Now Nineveh was an exceedingly great city, three days' journey in breadth. Jonah began to go into the city, going a day's journey. And he cried, "Yet forty days, and Nineveh shall be overthrown!" And the people of Nineveh believed God; they proclaimed a fast, and put on sackcloth, from the greatest of them to the least of them.

Then tidings reached the king of Nineveh, and he arose from his throne, removed his robe, and covered himself with sackcloth, and sat in ashes. And he made proclamation and published through Nineveh, "By the decree of the king and his nobles: Let neither man nor beast, herd nor flock, taste anything; let them not feed, or drink water, but let man and beast be covered with sackcloth, and let them cry mightily to God; yea, let every one turn from his evil way and from the violence which is in his hands. Who knows, God may yet repent and turn from his fierce anger, so that we perish not?"

When God saw what they did, how they turned from their evil way, God repented of the evil which he had said he would do to them; and he did not do it.

But it displeased Jonah exceedingly, and he was angry. And he prayed to the Lord, and said, "I pray thee, Lord, is not this what I said when I was yet in my country? That is why I made haste to flee to Tarshish; for I knew that thou art a gracious God and merciful, slow to anger, and abounding in steadfast love, and repentest of evil. Therefore now, O Lord, take my life from me, I beseech thee, for it is better for me to die than to live." And the Lord said, "Do you do well to be angry?" Then Jonah went out of the city and sat to the east of the city, and made a booth for himself there. He sat under it in the shade, till he should see what would become of the city.

And the Lord God appointed a plant, and made it come up over Jonah, that it might be a shade over his head, to save him from his discomfort. So Jonah was exceedingly glad because of the plant. But when dawn came up the next day, God appointed a worm which attacked the plant, so that it withered. When the sun rose, God appointed a sultry east wind, and the sun beat upon the head of Jonah so that he was faint; and he asked that he might die, and said, "It is better for me to die than to live." But God said to Jonah, "Do you do well to be angry for the plant?" And he said, "I do well to be angry, angry enough to die." And the Lord said, "You pity the plant, for which you did not labor, nor did you make it grow, which came into being in a night, and perished in a night. And should not I pity Nineveh, that great city, in which there are more than a hundred and twenty thousand persons who do not know their right hand from their left, and also much cattle?"

We shall discuss the last two chapters together because they form so close a unity that to split them is arbitrary. Furthermore, we shall find to some extent the same themes as in the first chapter, but now transposed and clarified and with a different perspective on the relations between God and man. We shall thus follow the same divisions.

1. TWO MEN IN ME

From now on the striking feature of the story is the great debate between God and Jonah, a Jonah who is no longer a rebel and a fugitive from God's word, a Jonah who has really been baptized and converted, an obedient Jonah, a new creature whom God wants in his service. There is no doubt but that Jonah is now obeying the Holy Spirit. He agrees to convey this difficult word. He agrees to go to Nineveh. He gives up his own will and puts himself in God's hands. His conversion in hell in not a spurious one. He is charged with the word and he fulfills this charge at the risk of his life. But even after the new birth Jonah is still a man of flesh and blood. He is still in our image. He is not perfect. He is capable of anger, self-justification, and despair. He has not become a plaster saint.

In this sense the story of Jonah is for us both a lesson in humility and also a strong consolation. Often biblical passages leave the suggestion that after conversion everything is rosy, there are no more problems, one is automatically in tune with God's will, one obeys without effort, one brings forth the fruits of sanctity as a tree bears its fruits, it is not hard but sweet to do what God demands, one does not commit any more sins. To be sure,

Paul speaks of two men battling in him; Jonah shows it too. But this idea of sainthood in the Roman Catholic sense of moral perfection is often very discouraging when we note that our own lives are not at all like that. The new birth leaves us with our difficulties and adds new problems and we continue to be sinners. We thus come to doubt the reality of our conversion. We begin to think that we are the victims of an illusion, that nothing really happened. What Paul says about the conflict between the flesh and the Spirit seems very abstract, and often it is not very important for us unless—which is worse—it is taken to refer to the conflict between the body and the soul. In Jonah we see a man who is like us, who has reactions like ours, whose revolts and sins are ours. We have a live instance, full of psychological truth and great spiritual profundity, of the debate to which St. Paul refers.

This is of value to us so long as we do not try to use it to justify ourselves. What we have not to say is that after all Jonah was still disobedient even in his obedience, still a sinner even in his vocation, and why should not I be the same? He who speaks thus shows in truth that he has not had a true encounter with the almighty Lord. Jonah has nothing to say except to the humble, penitent, and stricken heart, the man who is not satisfied to remain a sinner and who does not seek justification but pardon. To this man alone does the sharp and cutting dialogue between God and Jonah carry a truth. It tells this man that God knows the totality of man, that he knows with whom he is dealing, that he is not surprised even after revelation and pardon have been granted to find a man who is angry and disputatious again, that this does not exhaust God's love and patience, that he continues to take this rebellious child by the hand until he falls on his knees: My Lord and my God! This will be repeated throughout the life of this man as often as is necessary, since there are no limits to the love of God which forgives seventy times seven, that is, infinitely. But this has nothing to say and has no truth except for the man who does not try to treat this love and forgiveness as a source of personal profit. May Jonah's sin be an aid to our repentance and not a justification in our pride!

* * * * *

Jonah proclaims the word, but when he sees that nothing happens as he has declared he is angry with God. He also finds here an argument to justify his earlier conduct. It was no good making me undertake this journey and incur all this risk for nothing. I told you so! God was wrong and Jonah right when Jonah wanted to go to Tarshish and not to Nineveh. Jonah is sufficiently in communion with God to see in the facts of his life the work of God, to find consolation in this, and to be appeased at the first sign of love God shows him (the gourd). And yet he is also the despairing sinner, despairing even to death, when he loses his consolation and help. He plunges again into anger and despair. He again says that he is right and God wrong.

I think that in this description we can discern many things which are of great value for personal edification.

First, Jonah incessantly tries to justify himself (4:2). "I knew very well," he says to God. He no longer needs grace. After all, what happened was all an accident. God did not know what he was doing. Why has he fetched back Jonah from the depths of the sea, why has he pursued him, when it all leads up to the miserable defeat of a Nineveh which is still standing and to which condemnation has done nothing? What seems to me to be the essential thing in Jonah's attitude, however, is the reason he gives for it; it is a spiritual justification: "I knew that thou art a gracious God and merciful, slow to anger, and abounding in steadfast love, and repentest of evil" (4:2). It was not worth it to send Jonah to Nineveh to announce its destruction when God is a God of love who does not condemn or destroy, when he could only pardon Nineveh. All he demanded of

Jonah was futile from the very first and even against nature.

Jonah thus uses revelation to dispute God's will. For he quotes the very words the Lord spoke to Moses, particularly solemn and sacred words which are at the very heart of revelation since God spoke them after making his covenant with the Jewish people through the mediation of Moses (Exodus 34:6). Jonah sets God against God, God's word against God's command, and all to justify himself. We have in Scripture at least one other example of this, when Satan comes into the wilderness to tempt Jesus and he, too, uses texts from the Bible: "It is written. . . ."

This is a grave warning; it is not enough to lean on a biblical text to be right; it is not enough to adduce biblical arguments, whether theological or pietistic, to be in tune with God. All this may denote opposition to God. It may even be a way of disobeying him. The using of God's word to tempt God is a danger which threatens all Christians. Every time the Christian thinks he has God's word in store to be used as needed, he commits this sin, which is that of Satan himself against Christ. This is the attitude of the historian who dissects Scripture to set it against Scripture, of the theologian who uses a text to construct his doctrine or philosophy, or of the simple Christian who opens his Bible to find himself justified there, or to find arguments against non-Christians or against Christians who do not hold the same views, arguments which show how far superior my position is to that of others. It is not for nothing the Bible shows us that this attitude of Jonah is that of Satan. As Peter immediately after his confession invites the rebuke: "Get behind me, Satan!" so Jonah after his conversion and the fulfilment of his mission is assimilated to Satan. This should stir us to great caution in the reading and use of the Bible. It is not a neutral book which one can read and then take arguments from it. It is an explosive power which must be handled with care.

But if the simple reading and use of this book are so

dangerous, our hearts are filled with fear. Is there nothing to save us from this terrible temptation? Of course there is, and the text itself gives it to us. Jonah uses Scripture to justify himself before God and against God, and this leads him to seek self-destruction. But here precisely is his condemnation. When we find in the Bible that which justifies us in our own eyes, when in reading the Bible we say: "I was right," when we see in it an argument for us and against others, when we are righteous in our own judgment, we can be certain that like Jonah we have turned the revelation against God. For what revelation teaches us about ourselves is all to the effect that we are not righteous, that we have no means of justifying ourselves, that we have no possibility of disputing with God, that we have no right to condemn others and be in the right against them, and that in this extreme distress only a gracious act of God which is external to us (though it becomes internal) can save us. This is what Scripture teaches us, and if we stick to this, reading the Bible is useful and healthy and brings forth fruit in us. It is the source of life and truly God's work, without which it necessarily becomes the source of death and Satan's work. After justifying himself Jonah says to God: "It is better for me to die than to live" (4:3).

* * * * *

Jonah is angry with God. He sins. He knew he was a prophet and bearer of God's word. He declared this word with seriousness, totality, and faithfulness. He risked his life and told these others that they were risking their lives and would perish. As God's ambassador he proclaimed God's will to them. He placed himself and them in the center of the greatest conflict where everything was involved. And now nothing has happened. The men of Nineveh go about their business, and politics and commerce resume after this emotional crisis: "life goes on."

What are the people of Nineveh going to think? Exactly what people of our world think of the Christian message.

How many times has the Church announced God's judgment and nothing has happened! One can no longer believe in it. How many times has the Church preached repentance in view of the divine anger and there has been no anger! What do they think of Jonah? He is a bluffer or a visionary. And what do men think of God? He is an impotent God, a ridiculous God, or better a non-existent God. Thus Jonah seems to have good reason for his anger, not just because his own pride is wounded but because God's pride is wounded. God's honor had been involved in this adventure too, and Jonah insists that the word spoken should be executed.

We have here an important point. Jonah demands that God obey the prophetic word about the world, that he be faithful to what he has said through his servant. And once again Jonah is obeying a human inclination, which is that of all the witnesses and of which there are other instances in Scripture, namely, to make God's word one's own word. The word is no longer to be respected because it is the free act of the God who speaks and it is done, of the God who remains free in his word. The word is now the word of Jonah. What Jonah has said counts. God is bound to the word of Jonah. Jonah finds it intolerable that God should maintain his freedom now that he, the prophet, has, in sum, personally guaranteed the revelation. That God should change his will is impossible in the eyes of man once man has adopted this will. Here again we find a common attitude of Christians and the Church. It is hard for us to submit to the freedom of God, to his faithfulness, which is far above our casuistry.

Furthermore, Jonah, obeying God's will, is among the righteous. He is the man who does God's will. He knows the drama of disobedience even to death. He has been vanquished by God. He is now in the camp of God's friends, the righteous. This has cost him dear and the sacrifices he has had to make are terrible. He now finds it normal and good that the rest, those who do not obey

God, those who lead their lives in the world as they wish, those who now scoff at this impotent God and his absurd prophet—it is normal and good that they should experience a little of the wrath of this God as Jonah has known it, that they should be put to death: then they would see! Jonah, now that he is among the righteous, finds it easy to divide the world into the saved and the lost, the righteous and sinners, the living and the dead. And since the men of Nineveh are lost and damned there is no reason for pity; they deserve to be, and this should be seen and known. Of what avail are so many efforts and sacrifices, so much loyalty, if the wicked who profit in a life which we renounce are not damned? Jonah with the good conscience he has newly acquired demands their condemnation.

We have here precisely the anger of the Jewish people against the Gentiles, the hope they will be damned. This anger existed prior to Jesus Christ, for historians believe that the Book of Jonah was rightly composed to affirm the universalism of salvation, to fight against the narrow nationalistic view, against the hatred of the Jews for the heathen. But this anger has increased with the dispersion and persecution of the Jewish people; vengeance will come from the Lord; the Gentiles heap coals of fire on their heads. And we find the same attitude in the Church. It is that of good Christians against pagans, of good moralists against sinners. It is the collective attitude of the Church when it preaches crusades or engages in wars of extermination (e.g., against the Indians of Brazil) or in the holy war against Communism. Jonah brings to light a contemporary attitude, our own.

At this point Jonah shows that he has not really understood his own adventure. He has understood only one thing, his own sacrifice and faithfulness. He has already forgotten the grace which was lavished on him. He has already lost the mystery of the pardon by which he lives anew in newness of life. For him everything depended on that grace, but he does not think it a good thing that it should be shown to others. He has already forgotten that if God's wrath was upon him, it was finally to show him grace, to pardon him.

Thus when he demands that God be faithful to the word spoken, that he do what he has said, he misses the point that God's faithfulness is higher than that. God is above all things faithful to his love, to his love for all men, sinners and pagans among the rest. If the Lord has had Jonah preach, it is with a view to the salvation of Nineveh and in faithfulness to his love for it. To achieve this salvation God has risked everything. Here he risks his honor. He places himself under the judgment of men. He is ready to be a figure of derision among them. He accepts their insults: "Look at this God who cannot do anything against us. Look at this God who can only talk. . . ." He accepts all this simply in order that these men might be saved. It is true that God cannot do anything against man. He is bound by his love. He can only seek to save them. But this degree of humiliation into which God in effect drags his servants is insupportable to Jonah; he has too high a view of God's dignity. God, however, does not locate his dignity at the same point as man does. He does not locate his faithfulness in the formalism which his servant would require when he applies the word himself.

Jonah, being angry, leaves the city. This is the normal reaction. If God will not keep his word, at least Jonah will keep his. He wants nothing more to do with this accursed city. He leaves and sits down to the east of it in a booth to see what will happen, for he is still persuaded that things cannot go on as they are. He separates himself; he wants to show in this way that he is a saint (a separated one) in the very face of this city and in opposition to it. His gesture is also that of a prophet. He sits to the east, the place from which God's judgment comes. By the very place he thus shows that he expects this judgment, just as we in our churches await the day of judgment, not the day of grace but that of God's wrath on the world. Jonah separates

himself to show his own righteousness. This is undoubtedly demanded sometimes: "Come out from among
them. . . ." But this is not what is asked of Jonah. He has
been sent to the city to be in its midst, to be with it, to
share its judgment, repentance, and salvation. He has been
sent to convey grace and not damnation. Thus the Church,
as leaven in the lump which is of no value apart from the
lump, can serve no useful purpose if it installs itself outside
the world.

Jonah sits in the shade of the booth which he has made.
This is a curious situation for a servant of God. There is
threefold disobedience. He has in fact no right to install
himself either in the grace he has been shown or the
function he has been given. He has no right, before God, to
come to a halt and say: "It is done." God's work is never
done. It is impossible for God's servant to take his ease
before God as though this were the right thing. He is a man
marching to a new country, a man with no attachments or
roots in this world, a man who is always a stranger and
pilgrim on earth, returning to the Lord. The material
attitude of Jonah is characteristic of his spiritual self-justification. He sits down because he thinks he has taken
possession of the world and discharged his function.

Jonah sits in the shade of the booth he has made. The
peace he finds is self-given. He neither seeks nor awaits
God's protection and grace. God's question: "Do you do
well to be angry?" (4:4) he rejects and will not listen to,
for he creates his own domain in the shade where he will
be at peace according to his own measure, just as
Christians try to make a church according to their own
measure—it is not the body of Christ—and a divine
kingdom according to their own measure, full of intentions
which are good and effective and well constructed, but
which are only a fresh demonstration of their autonomy in
relation to God.

In the shade of the booth Jonah is far from the sun and
equally far from God's question. His booth helps him not

to hear a phrase which ought to have had many associations for him since he was such a student of Scripture. It is in effect the same question as that which God put to Cain. When Cain, in face of the first act of God's good will, the acceptance of Abel's sacrifice, becomes angry and is full of envy and murder, God says to him too: "Why are you angry?" and at that moment Cain decides to become a murderer, so that it is not for nothing the question is repeated here. Jonah, too, is angered by God's benevolence and he demands the execution of the threat, the slaying of the people of Nineveh. Hence he, too, becomes a fratricide. He even asks God to take part in murder. He becomes Cain, for he is in truth the brother of these people in his revolt, his condemnation, and the pardon he receives. At this point we too, the Church, must be very careful. When we have a sense of our own righteousness, when we hope for or desire God's judgment on sinners and rebels, this simple verse teaches us that we range ourselves alongside Cain, and that it was not for this that Jesus Christ came.

But even this thought does not prick Jonah, so sure is he that he is on the side of right. Sitting there, he waits to see what will happen. He becomes a spectator. He is now outside the action. He looks, hoping that Nineveh will be destroyed by fire and its inhabitants grilled, like those who wait for the judgment when the world will be finally destroyed and we, the pious, will see the wicked punished, though in fact the warning that we should not look for the day of the Lord, since it will be one of terror and wrath, is addressed to the pious.

In this passivity Jonah is guilty of a third betrayal. He was never discharged. He has no right to look. Onlookers are not loved by the crucified Savior. There is an exact parallel to Jonah's situation in the life of Abraham. Here again a city was to be destroyed. But Abraham as God's servant fights desperately to save it from condemnation. He prays to God six times. He does not isolate himself from the destiny of the city, even though it is not his own.

He cannot accept judgment on men. He involves himself to the limit to save it. He cannot stand the spectacle of the furnace. And at the very last Lot leaves the city, but those who turn back to look are condemned.

Thus Jonah continues his disobedience just because he wants to be faithful. His desire is to be a true servant, but he has not yet grasped the infinite dimension of God's love.

He waits to see what will happen. He is sure in his own mind that what will happen will be the condemnation of Nineveh. But the story goes on to tell us that what happens is something very different. God sends up a plant, a gourd, which grows above Jonah's head. God does this to appease the anger of Jonah, and Jonah is indeed very pleased. It is quite different from what he expected. It is the precise opposite. Instead of being an act against Nineveh it is an act on behalf of Jonah. And one must say that he had need of it, for in new revolt he was close to condemnation himself. But no, God once again shows his love. He decides once more to save Jonah and to appease him. He gives him a sign of his grace.

This sign, the gourd, has greatly troubled exegetes. For one thing they cannot identify it. A connection has been suggested with the Egyptian *kiki* and this has led some to propose an Egyptian origin for the book, but there is more of imagination than there is of fact in such conjectures. Nor is the matter of the least importance; we may accept the mystery. The important thing is that the plant is a visible sign of grace. But then a second problem arises for exegetes. Jonah had made a booth for shade, but now God causes the gourd to grow "to be a shade over his head" (4:6) and when it withers he is left in the open sun again. What happened to his booth? All kinds of exegetical hypotheses have been advanced, and in despair some have argued that we really have two stories (one about the booth and the other about the gourd) which have become confused or have been badly copied. In sum, the present text is the result of an error. These redactors of the books of the Bible must have been really stupid to perpetrate and perpetuate such gross mistakes! But is there not an explanation once we admit that the book was written, not to tell a logical story, but to record a spiritual revelation? We then see that the text has been edited with great care, as is apparent, for example, in the echoing of Cain's question. Jonah made a booth to get shade and peace. But we have seen that the prophet no longer has this mastery over his life. Hence God replaces the shade he has made by a tree. He replaces the peace Jonah has given himself by his own peace: "My peace I give to you; not as the world gives do I give to you." In other words, by substituting the plant for the booth God puts his servant back in the true position of the servant. He takes away the false constructions which he had made, and in truth made against God. He takes away his false security. He replaces it by the sign of grace which (in and by God's will) ensures true security, which presupposes the putting of his destiny in the hands of the Lord (so that it ceases to be destiny), and also true joy.

There is no exegetical problem as between the booth and the gourd; there is a spiritual problem.

* * * * *

Jonah was in doubt and despair. His anger alone was not enough to explain the fact that twice he wanted death: the first time when he realized that God was not going to destroy Nineveh, and he asked that he might die. I think we need to understand this extreme chagrin. Here we do not merely have a vexed or humiliated man; both times he is in despair. He is so because it seems that all he has believed is called in question. He doubts. We have to see Jonah's situation as it is, in our own reality, as it might be in our own lives. Jonah received a mission from God. He passed through terrible adventures before yielding. He finally received grace. He experienced the new birth. God worked in his life; he consecrated this life to God. He acts according to God's word. But nothing happens! What God has said does not come to pass. And when he prays that God will fulfill his word, God does not hear his prayer.

Inevitably, then, Jonah comes under the test of satanic temptation, the test of Eve in the garden: "Did God say...?" Jonah no longer has a material sign of this grace and vocation. Had God really spoken to him? Was it really a call he received? Supposing it was a mistake? Supposing it was an illusion of his own brain or senses? What if God did not speak? Jonah cannot answer these questions. He undoubtedly has his adventures, his descent into the sea and the miracle of the fish (the death and resurrection of Jesus), but supposing this made no spiritual sense, supposing it might be explained rationally without God's intervention, supposing it was all chance or all on the human level? (Supposing Jesus swooned, or his disciples did actually steal the body? If we have faith in Christ only for this life, we are the most miserable of all men. Jonah is the most miserable of all men when subjected to this question.) And there is even good reason to think this might be so, for in the last resort how can we ever imagine that God would go to such pains to make Jonah obey, that he would raise up the tempest, the monster, etc., merely to achieve nothing, nothing at all, since the word of God is not fulfilled and Nineveh is not destroyed?

For Jonah, then, his spiritual experience, his new birth, his promised resurrection were all illusion. Nothing had changed in his life. There had been no decisive act of God. He had thought he was a new creature but he was still the same rebellious and desperate Jonah. He had thought he was in communion with God but God did not hear his prayer. He had thought he was a servant of God but obviously God did not approve of his services. He had risked his life and it was for nothing. One can understand Jonah's despair. It reached to the very heart of his life. What had become the most important thing was put in doubt. The purpose of his life slipped away through his fingers. He had indeed no further reason to live.

One can also see why the growth of the gourd brought him such joy. He saw it for what it was—a sign of God's grace. All was not lost. God was still with him. Here was proof he was not abandoned. Here was confirmation of all that had gone before. But when the gourd dies, we have exactly the same drama. Jonah grasped the sign without realizing that the grace of God lasts and persists even when the sign disappears. Because of the sign, grace seemed sure and certain to him, and when the sign disappeared grace became uncertain. This is the kind of movement we constantly go through. When the plant died Jonah began to ask again whether he had not regarded as a sign of grace something which really was not, whether he had not attributed to God a purely natural phenomenon, and therefore whether he was not abandoned now as he had been before. But God does not condemn Jonah. Jonah wants to die. He shows in this way that he clings to God's grace more than to life, that the only thing that matters for him is to be in communion with God, that his joy and life depend on this alone. In his extreme doubt and despair, he shows his love of God, and so God responds and helps him to understand the reality of his will and love.

These fluctuations, these dramas, this psychology of Jonah teaches us about ourselves. First, we are brought back, as we have seen, to this co-existence of two men, to the survival of the carnal man in spite of the new birth; we need not pursue this. Also implied is the fact that the man chosen by God is far from having plumbed the full depths of God's mysteries. Jonah is ignorant about many things, and especially that God wants the salvation of the sinner and not his death, that God is love and not just the implacable opponent who has pursued him. Jonah does not know this. Thus the man chosen by God knows about God only what God has willed to reveal to him. The man filled with the Holy Spirit knows only a small part of the mysteries and even of the action of God. The adventure of Jonah inclines us at every point to humility.

We have also to see that we cannot stop at the point of the new birth. When he came forth from the fish Jonah understood many things; he had decided to obey God; he had entered into communion with him. But he stopped there. His vocation filled his whole spiritual horizon. It is the same with us; whether through laziness or enthusiasm, we try to stop at the same spiritual experience where, it seems, we received everything and understood everything. In effect Jonah judges everything in relation to this first fulness and does not see that he is just beginning a long way, like a newborn infant who does not realize that his life will not just be the moment when life was manifested independently in him but is the unfolding of time for him.

It is impossible to stop at the day of creation or to want to do so, just as it was impossible for Peter to make booths on the top of the mountain and to stay forever with the transfigured Jesus. Nor can we build on this first experience or all the others which might follow. When we try to build on our spiritual experiences, on the facts in our lives which we see to be of God, we oscillate like Jonah between joy and doubt, for we are never certain of what we have lived through or of the interpretation we have given it. We may have conflicting experiences like Jonah. We may thus regard all that is positive in our lives as illusion. We must not build on what happens to us personally. We can indeed regard certain things in our lives as signs, miracles, God's particular and personal action on us. But we are then to move on to what is signified by them. We must not cling to the sign itself, even though it be the most beautiful mystical experience. We must leave behind what belongs to the past. We must fix our regard on what caused the sign, on what is shown us by it.

All the uncertainties which might result from subjective experiences disappear if instead of stopping at them we refer them to God, if it is God who counts and not our experiences. Jonah had met God. But if he is truly fixed on him, why be shattered when the sign of the gourd vanishes, when the sign gives place to the reality? This wounds us, of course, in our subjectivity. The miracle gives a pleasant sense of personal contact with God. To refer all to God, to count on God's patience and love, to respect his freedom, to love his will—all this objectivity sometimes leaves us cold when we ought to be reassured by it and confident, since we are placing our very doubts on certainty.

In the Book of Jonah God's final answer is precisely to this effect. This time God does not give a personal, subjective sign; he gives an objective reply about Nineveh. As in Job, God reveals himself to Jonah objectively, in his power and his love. This objective revelation is what ought to calm Jonah by forcing him to take a further step, to leave his subjectivity, to find his true and total center in the permanence and faithfulness of the love of God.

2. THE PATIENCE OF GOD

The strategy of God which we spoke of in the first chapter lies in his patience in a twofold sense. God waits, tolerates, and pursues until the moment when man is convinced. God puts up with man's excuses and delays in obeying and living. This patience of God is an extraordinary testimony to his love. In love God recommences indefinitely the work which man bungles. God seeks to make himself loved by man, to save man. He uses every means. He employs all his understanding and long-suffering and hope. He is never discouraged. He never stops remaking and forgiving. But God also knows what he is doing. He knows where he wants to lead man. When Jonah is cast out on dry land, God does not congratulate him. He hardly leaves him time to catch his breath. He speaks his word: "Arise, go to Nineveh and proclaim to it the message that I tell you" (3:2). Nothing has changed from the very beginning. God's will has not altered. The great events which have transpired, the fish and the monster, are only episodes. What remains is what God demands. The order given to Jonah is the same as at the first moment. All that has happened relates to this order.

In every change and circumstance God is the same. His purpose is the same. Every time we get the impression of a change in God's will, every time we see striking contradictions, we must realize that these are only in our imperfect view of God's will, in our own subjectivity. Thus we can receive a particular command or a precise call from God. In consequence of the call we may be enmeshed in adventures which seem to be open to condemnation even from God's standpoint. This is one of the great shelters in ethical discussions among Protestant Christians. Every time a general principle is enunciated there is at once added: "But of course God can issue calls which contradict this command." Jonah takes shelter in this. Against the divine order to declare the destruction of Nineveh he sets the great revelation that God is rich in goodness, that God does not want to destroy the world. What Jonah does not see is that there is no contradiction here. To reconcile God's general will to save and his particular will that Jonah should be a prophet of destruction is not always easy, or rather, it is easy when we look back. We then see that in effect there was no contradiction, that the surprising command of God was part of a totality which corresponds perfectly with his revelation. But often the call seems dubious. What we have always to realize in any case is that when God gives an order he stands by it.

God's objectivity cuts across our subjectivities. The faithfulness of God makes up for our inconstancies. God alone knows the general strategy in which each specific vocation has its own place. But we can count on his faithfulness and know that if we are truly obedient we have no need to pass judgment on our vocation. God will extract from it the good he thinks necessary.

But this persistence in the command, this renewal of it, also teaches us that Jonah, in spite of the spiritual experience he had had, in spite of the knowledge of grace he had gained, in spite of his decision to be faithful, did not become free to select for himself what he would say to men. He did not go to them to tell them about his experiences or the revelations he might have had. He did not decide on the content of his preaching. God did not tell him to go to Nineveh to say what he thought was good. God commanded the same preaching. Thus, no matter what our spiritual development may be, our witness is fast bound to the word of God. The greatest saint or mystic can say nothing of value unless it is based solely on God's word. "Even if . . . an angel from heaven should preach to you another gospel," you are not to believe him, and what is true in relation to the individual is also true in relation to the Church. The Church is not to choose its preaching. It must simply follow as faithfully as possible the eternal order and the *hic et nunc* order of its Lord.

* * * * *

Finally, when God renews his order to Jonah, this tells us plainly that Jonah is an instrument in God's hands. God needs man. He may sometimes act *ex nihilo* with no intermediary, but in fact this is rare. God is not one who despises man. He is the one who elevates man to the dignity in which he has a part in God's work. He is the one who patiently waits for man's assent to do this work. Naturally God could have saved Nineveh without Jonah's preaching. But a mysterious salvation in which man had no part at all and of which he had no knowledge would be an expression of supreme contempt for man. When God chose Jonah he wanted his people (the Church) to have a part in the salvation decided for Nineveh. This shows that the call of Jonah, God's patience with him, the pursuit, the order given, the grace accorded, the conversion, were not for Jonah's sake but for the sake of Nineveh. We sometimes confer too great importance on our individual spiritual or religious life. To be sure, each of us is of infinite worth before God, for he gave his Son to save us. But above all each of us is important for the work which God demands. The Christian is not just the man who is saved by Christ; he is the man whom God uses for the salvation of others by Christ.

It is absolutely necessary that Nineveh be warned, that it be given a choice, that it be saved from its sin. It is necessary because God has so decided. It is also necessary that the people which carries revelation do this work. Who else could do it? It is thus necessary that Jonah, the messenger, carry the message. The special care which God takes of Jonah is finally, then, his care for the salvation of Nineveh. If Jonah receives a call, if he is truly saved, it is for others. From the moment faith develops in us, we must be permeated by the conviction that if grace is conferred on us it is primarily for others. It is never for our own personal satisfaction. Our salvation and our adventure are functions of the salvation and adventure of the men around us, and ultimately of the world. The Christian is thus necessarily involved, not just in work for the salvation of his immediate neighbors, but also in God's global work. It cannot be otherwise, for God is love and he establishes relations of love wherever he passes by. This is what Jonah did not grasp the first time, but God's patience led him to accept it.

* * * * *

Jonah thus goes to Nineveh and declares: "Yet forty days, and Nineveh shall be overthrown!" (3:4). The number forty is significant, like almost all the numbers of the Bible. We must not fall into allegory but at the same time we must not suppress what is part of revelation. I know that a dangerous path opens up before us here, but perhaps it is not wholly useless. As regards the significance of numbers one might follow the classical methods of the rabbis in which each Hebrew number is represented by letters, and thus the meaning of the letters is sought and by analogy one gets the meaning of the digit or number. This seems to me to be most insecure, though preferable to the fantasies of M. Abélio, who follows a so-called secret teaching. This alchemy leads only to vague mystical speculations representing once again man's attempt to seize revelation for his own use. There will be nothing of that here. We shall try to see clearly from Scripture's own use what is signified by the number forty.

If we consult the accounts in which forty plays a role, we first find that they are very numerous, then that they all have the same bearing. In fact, we can group them in two parallel series. The first contains the forty days of the flood, when rain covered the earth and the abyss regained possession of the earth. Then when Moses had slain the Egyptian, and thus failed in his mission to bring back the people to the Lord, and also to deliver it, because he did not rely solely on God's power, he had to wait forty years before he could take up his path again according to God's word revealed to him at the burning bush. A similar delay of forty years was inflicted on the Jewish people in the wilderness when it rebelled, when it refused to obey God, to trust in him for entry into the land of promise. Then when Elijah thought he was the only servant of the Lord left, when he was convinced the religion of the true God was at an end and the powers of the state would carry the day, he fled both to save his life and also to meet the Lord, and journeyed for forty days. Finally, we recall that Jesus at the beginning of his ministry was sent into the desert to be tempted by Satan, and this was for forty days.

It may be seen quite readily that the period here denotes a time of testing. One might say that God suspends his wrath, that he exercises patience to give man a chance by which he might profit or which he might reject, but which carries the risk of bringing down on him God's wrath. The striking thing about this series of texts, however, is that the delay in God's wrath and judgment always has a favorable outcome. Noah is saved, Moses becomes the leader of God's people, Israel enters Palestine, Elijah returns when he learns there are seven thousand men who have not bowed the knee to Baal, Jesus overcomes the temptation and angels minister to him. We know of no instance where the forty days or years do not lead to salvation. This throws an astonishing light not only on the present text but also on God's patience. It seems that in this testing delay man's will is already converted, already turned to God. It seems the test was successful from the very first. It seems the thing asked of man is simply acceptance and fulfilment of something which was already a reality.

This is in full agreement with the second series of passages which cite the number. The main ones are as follows: First, the waters of the flood take forty days to go down; included here is the story of the dove which comes back with the sign of salvation and the new covenant. Then when Moses becomes leader of the people of Israel he climbs Mt. Sinai and remains hidden in the clouds and thunderings, in God's presence, for forty days; when he comes down his face is so resplendent with the divine glory that he has to put on a veil. Again, when the people is on the point of entering Canaan it gets an order to send secret envoys or spies to inspect the land and visit the towns and to report on what they find; these spies stay there for forty days. Then the reigns of David and Solomon, which in different ways are prophetic of the reign of Christ, both last for forty years. Finally, the period between the resurrection and the ascension is one of forty days. The number thus refers to the establishment of the covenant (both old and new), but it denotes a particular aspect of it. It is the time when God's kingdom is set up on earth in a way which is hidden but beyond dispute for those who have eyes to see. It is the time of a new humanity with Noah, obedient to the Lord's will. It is the time of God's taking possession of his people by giving them the laws on Sinai. It is the time of the hidden and symbolical but nonetheless true and certain possession of the land of Canaan by the envoys of God. It is the time of

91

the prophetic affirmation of the reign of Jesus Christ in David and Solomon; these two figures of Jesus Christ both reveal and conceal his reality. Finally, it is the time of the presence on earth of the glorious and risen body of the Lord who will return in this body to establish his reign; it is a true and hidden affirmation of this reign.

If we go on to combine the two series of passages we can say that they explain one another (as we have already said that they are parallel). In effect they do not have two contradictory or separate meanings but two complementary meanings. The trial delay imposed by God is designed in the long run to manifest God's present and actual rule. Conversely, this rule is itself a decisive test for man, since it puts him against the wall where he must make a definitive decision, deciding for God and entering his kingdom.

Jonah is thus a prophet when he gives this breathing-space to the men of Nineveh. But he acts like a prophet in the current popular sense of one who says what is going to happen. He undoubtedly does not grasp the sense of his own words. When he declares: "Yet forty days . . . " he does not realize what he is saying; these words are given to him by the Holy Spirit. If he had known he would not have been surprised by what actually happened; he would not have rebelled at it. In effect these simple words presuppose that there is a trial delay for Nineveh in face of God's rule and with a view to it—a delay which, not fatalistically but according to the symbolism of the Bible, will lead to Christ, to man's assent to God's will. Jonah is thus declaring to Nineveh: "You are in the presence of the lordship of God, you will repent, and you will manifest thereby this rule of God among you." This is in effect what happens. God as it were takes possession of Nineveh and in these forty days of repentance he shows that he is truly the Lord; the fact that the king himself submits and orders the fast draws attention to this.

We do not forget that Nineveh is the world. This is the

point of the whole story. But the rule thus revealed can only be transitory. It is not visible to us. It is only prophetic of what is there already in hidden form but will later be total and evident. This is why there is no further question of this conversion of Nineveh in the course of history, just as there is no further question of the bodily presence of the risen Christ in the world in the course of our history.

This raises again the problem of the seriousness of Nineveh's conversion. Obviously this is a serious conversion which intimates God's kingdom. But it can only intimate it and not establish it. Hence it is not a conversion which is inscribed in history and is of perpetual duration. But it still ensures the salvation of Nineveh.

* * * * *

All this brings us to the very heart of God's patience. In reality God bears it that man is a sinner. He abhors sin, but he cannot accept the loss of man. He detests evil just because it is this which deflects man from life and plunges him into death and suffering. This is also why he endures the sinner. He will not simply blot him out. It began with Adam. God renounced his power and justice rather than condemning Adam at once. He also respects the sinner. He treats him as a creature, a man. (God treats man much better than he treats himself in his Son and much better than man treats himself—that is love!) He appeals to his will, his choice, his love. God gives man time for this, all the time he needs. God rejoices when man finally changes direction and returns to fellowship with the Father.

From this angle the story of God's decision about Nineveh adds certain elements. To God sin is ignorance, monumental, fundamental, and yet also monstrous ignorance: "persons who do not know their right hand from their left" (4:11). This is an uncommon view of sin in Scripture. But it is not opposed to the classical view. This is what Jesus is saying when he has compassion on the crowds which wander like sheep without a shepherd. Here, too, we are in the presence of men who do not know what they ought to do and who commit sin because they cannot discern between real good and real evil. This is the effect of the disobedience of Adam, which was meant to give man this knowledge of good and evil in himself. Man has no knowledge at all. Yet the distinction is obvious and St. Paul (Romans 1 and 2) shows how obvious it is. It is just as obvious as the distinction between the right hand and the left, the text says. But man's eyes are now closed to this obvious distinction because instead of seeing good and evil in relation to God, as God sees and distinguishes them, he now sees them in himself and as he decides.

The inhabitants of Nineveh had a very complex religion. They had a morality which, while not ours, was quite valid from the human standpoint, and helped them to discern between what they called good and what they called evil. They had a powerful state which for its part issued commands representing the good, and disobedience to these commands was punished by death because to disobey was evil. In this structure, as the Ninevites were not much worse than we are, they had the impression of doing good, for in the main they followed the precepts of their religion, morality, and state. In all this they were much like us.

Yet God teaches us that all this is to no effect; they do not really know good and evil. They do evil without realizing it, but it is still evil. And the presence of evil is intolerable to God. Though they are not aware of it, their wickedness before God is great: "their wickedness has come up before me" (1:2). Their ignorance does not excuse it nor diminish their responsibility; in the Bible responsibility is not tied to knowledge. They belong to the realm of Satan, and because of this they are condemned.

Man drags down the animals into this condemnation too. They are not responsible but they are bound to their fallen masters. They are engulfed in the impending destruction. Fallen man is still king and head of creation;

94

he reigns over it and makes it follow his way. But animals, too, count before God. He did not create them for the abyss. He does not neglect them in the work of salvation. It is for them too that redemption is achieved. Saved man brings with him the animals of which he is king. Before God man and animals are considered together and saved together.

Because of their ignorance, erring, striving, and seeking, God pities them as Jesus has compassion on the crowds. Because of their striving and seeking! This text itself suggests this: "You pity the plant, for which you did not labor. . . . And should not I pity Nineveh, that great city. . ?" (4:10, 11), implying that it has cost a great deal of trouble, that men have suffered, worked, and searched on its behalf. God thus takes man's labor into account even though it is labor in sin and it participates in evil. God takes seriously what man does, for he loves man totally, and hence with his work too. God has compassion. God sends Jonah because he has compassion. In his love he has decided to save this great city, the world.

This is not at all because the men of Nineveh do not know good and evil, are not responsible, and hence cannot be condemned. To see things thus is to open the door again to man's pride, to ensure his immunity, his independence in relation to God. God pities them because they are in misery. In spite of their army, technical skill, administration, and religion, they are in misery, for according to God there is no greater misery than that of not discerning between good and evil. In spite of their state and king they are without a shepherd, for there is no leader in whom one may fully trust apart from the absolutely just Lord who is also absolutely merciful.

The men of our age know this well. They are constantly condemned for their loyalty to the state when the state changes hands, just as members of the Communist Party can be condemned for their very loyalty to Communism and by their own chiefs. If they are pitied, this depends

95

solely on God, and all man's salvation depends on this pity of God. If God ceased to pity, there could be no exit from our hell. But God does not cease to pity because he is love.

God sends Jonah to set the world before true good and evil. Jonah in effect declares the separation which exists between God and men, and this separation brings death to man. Jonah is sent to force Nineveh to an awareness of its true situation. Going beyond traditional rules of morality and state power, going beyond human certainties, Jonah sets Nineveh and its government and its animals before God's will. It is only before this will of God that man can know the evil that is in him and also the reality of good. Only before this intransigence of the divine justice can man learn to see that all that he has thus far considered good is really loss for him (Philippians 3:7). The preaching of Jonah is dramatically simple. In a striking way he declares the judgment and death of Nineveh. In a mysterious and hidden way (even for him) he announces its pardon. But Nineveh can grasp the pardon only by accepting its condemnation. Hence, this is no preaching of morality. Jonah does not say: Stop massacring prisoners or waging war. It is the preaching of a decision of God. He places Nineveh before God's will.

And this decision should have appeared to Nineveh both gratuitous and unreasonable. One might even say that to announce the decision ought to have provoked the mirth of the inhabitants. They were the supreme military power, victors over Babylon and Egypt; they feared nobody, and to talk of the destruction of Nineveh was fanciful from the human standpoint. But just because this was the preaching of God's word and not that of a seer or an essay in political prevision, Nineveh was set before a revelation, not before a probable or improbable fact. The only point at this juncture was to know if Nineveh would see in this preaching political (and seditious) propaganda, an act of opposition to the government, the words of a madman, an expression of economic interests, the declaration of an expert, or a word expressing a decision of God.

In the former case, the revolutionary might be put to death, the maniac locked up, or the expert opinion debated. In the latter, the only course is to be ready to enter the way of repentance, to accept the decision because it is God's, not because it is just or good or seems reasonable, nor because it is true, but solely because it is God's.

In man's eyes and by man's standards, God's decision always seems unjust, unreasonable, or debatable.

All the odds were that Nineveh would resist the preaching. We are here in the presence of a mystery and miracle. Nineveh does not react as one might expect from the human standpoint. In face of authentic preaching of the word, there is an absolutely unpredictable element in man's reactions. It is useless to try to go beyond this and to see who takes the first step or whether there is any merit. This is the mystery of God's presence at the heart of his creation in spite of the fall. All that we can know is that God makes the first step revealed to us. This step is God's compassion.

Nineveh thus recognizes a word of God and repents. This is not for social and humanitarian reasons, nor for reasons of conscience, but solely by reason of the fact that within the time granted to it Nineveh is placed before God's will and recognizes it as such. To God's decision comes the response of Nineveh's decision. It is only a response, and a response which signifies that Nineveh condemns itself, that it ceases in effect to be Nineveh. This repentance is not the vain formulation of pious repetitions. It is not regret. It is a hope, as the text says quite firmly (3:9). It is a hope which burgeons because man changes. Nineveh with its wholly war-like orientation accuses itself of violence (3:8). This means that what it has thus far been it sees to be evil. Nineveh, proud of its power and invincibility, ceases to be itself when it thus humbles itself.

"So that we perish not"—this is the precise point of God's patience.

It is also the point of our life. Our time is just the space God gives us to live. This time is given us because of God's patience. This patience awaits repentance, our repentance. The years allotted to us on earth can have no other possible meaning or orientation. The point is that all our life should be to God's glory and in his kingdom.

* * * * *

When Nineveh repents, God repents too: "God repented of the evil which he had said he would do to them; and he did not do it" (3:10). This is a surprising term to be used of God, and yet it is a common one in Scripture. God decides something, and then events change. Thus God changes his mind. He repents. It is useless to avoid the difficulty this causes by saying it is only a manner of speaking. Philosophers say that God cannot change. True enough! But the God revealed in Scripture is not the God of the philosophers. Nor can one attribute this to primitive characteristics in the people of Israel. Historians call this a gross anthropomorphism and one must not take it too seriously. To be sure it is an anthropomorphism. But God is not the God of the historians. To be noted first in relation to this repenting is that God repents of the evil he was going to do but never repents of the good. This general rule is formulated by St. Paul (Romans 2) and it is confirmed by a survey of the texts. Only once to my knowledge do we read that God repented of the good that he had done, and this is explained more by literary than theological considerations. In effect this repenting takes place only when there is the risk of some evil, some human suffering.

Again it is no doubt important to emphasize that the same Hebrew words are not used for the repentance of Nineveh and God's repenting. In a general way Scripture has different terms for man's repentance and the Lord's repenting. As concerns man, *shubh* implies a change, a

98

modification in attitude and direction (a conversion) in his very being, as we have seen. As concerns God, the word *nacham* is the usual term, and this does not imply a change of direction but inner suffering which must be consoled. It is suffering not because of self but because of the relation between self and others. This can happen in the relation between God and man, whether because man does not respond to God's appeal or because God's justice necessarily demands man's condemnation. The just and perfectly holy God condemns, and can do no other, but when man repents, when man changes, God suffers for having condemned him. One cannot say absolutely that he suppresses the condemnation. For in effect God does not change. What is done is done. What God has decided he has decided, the more so as it is decided for all eternity. When it is said that God repents, it means that he suffers, not that he changes what his justice has deemed necessary.

Now God's justice has deemed condemnation necessary because of past sin. Repentance alone does not efface the past. Once committed, a guilty act remains so even after repentance. Condemnation cannot be automatically lifted. There is no immanent mechanism. Repentance, an act of man, does not suppress the sins man has committed. The two are not in balance. What is between them is the fact that God repents, that he suffers and finds consolation.

But we must be more precise as to the meaning of this suffering. It is not just sentiment. It is not regret for having condemned. It is not a kindly thought which causes God to lift the condemnation, which would imply a change of attitude. Most of the passages which speak of God repenting say that he repents of the evil he had resolved to do. He suffers the evil, and not just because of the evil, but the evil itself. We might say with truth that God suffers the evil he has resolved to do. He takes upon himself the evil which was the wages of man's sin. He suffers the very suffering which in his justice he should have laid on man. God causes the judgment to fall on himself; this is the meaning of his repenting. We shall see that it is in Jesus Christ that this is done plainly and for us. Jesus Christ is precisely the one upon whom falls all the judgment and all the suffering decided for each of us, the judgment and the suffering of the world. In reality God's repenting in the face of man's repentance is Jesus Christ. Each time there is any question of this repenting in Scripture we thus have a new prophecy of Jesus Christ who puts into effect both the justice of God and also the love of God without doing despite to either the one or the other.

It is only from the perspective of human judgment that there seems to be a change in God's attitude. When the Lord proclaims condemnation and then does not fulfill it, we tend to say, if we are believers, that he has changed his will, and if we are not believers, that there is no God. But this is a purely temporal way of looking at it because we are not able to see Jesus in agony to the end of the world. God's purpose has not changed. From the very beginning his aim is to save the world from his own wrath.

3. THE THIRD PROPHECY

In the debate between Jonah and God concerning Nineveh Jonah is exactly like the wicked servant in the parable of Jesus. His master has forgiven him the great debt he owed, and from this interview in which he experienced his master's kindness he goes away only to seize a man who owes him a trifling sum and to exact payment. This is the very thing which has come to light in the preceding study. Yet not by a long way does it exhaust the sense of the chapters. For they are prophecy. They are in fact prophetic in that they reveal another aspect of the work of Jesus Christ, announcing it in advance as a witness.

What we have said thus far about God's patience explains the rather singular form of the prophecy, since this rests on God's patience. The decisive thing in the third prophecy is the parallelism between the two parts of the story. We are often tempted to read the biblical stories like novels, in linear fashion, as though events in a series were simply attached to one another by the flow of time and their reciprocal causality. Thus the story of Jonah is that of a man who receives a command to go to Nineveh, who disobeys, who is forced by God to obey, who goes, but whose word is not fulfilled, since Nineveh repents. When the story is viewed thus, even with its embellishments (as in most biblical histories), there is no grasp at all of its spiritual meaning. The story has to be taken as a significative (and not just a chronological) totality. It has to be taken synthetically, with the internal connections which join the various parts. In a way which is the exact opposite of this, exegetes say that we have two stories which bear little relation to one another. First there is the story of Jonah and then that of Nineveh. Except that the hero of both is called Jonah it is hard to see any connection between them.

In contrast it seems to me that the connection is very close and that it is precisely this which constitutes the third prophecy. Jonah is a man who does not obey God's will. Nor does Nineveh. Jonah is plunged into condemnation and hell; Nineveh is confronted with imminent condemnation. Jonah repents, and Nineveh fasts. Jonah is saved by grace, Nineveh is pardoned by grace. One can say in truth that what happened to Jonah in the first part of the story is reproduced exactly in what happens to Nineveh in the second part. We also remember that it was through Jonah as intermediary that Nineveh went through this experience. Jonah, a foreigner in Nineveh, coming to it from the elect people, went through the same experiences as Nineveh. He trod the path on which Nineveh would follow him when Jonah had brought it God's word. What happened to him happens to this great city. There is in fact a fellowship of destiny between them. In the long run what took place in Jonah's life takes place in that of every man. The salvation granted to Jonah from the depths of hell is what God has decided for all. Thus Jonah in his adventure, in his very life, proclaims the decision of salvation which is for all.

But it is essential that Jonah come first, that he experience this series of events first. We also see that when Nineveh follows him on the stages of his life its experiences are much less extreme and do not go as far as those of Jonah. But the same grace is shown to them, the same salvation is granted. The salvation of Nineveh is first given to Jonah. In some measure it depends on that of Jonah.

But if we consider the story only in its human dimension, what we have just said is not necessarily true. In any case it is not significant. We might interpret it very simply: Jonah had to undergo this experience in order to fulfill his role in relation to Nineveh. In fact, however, we have to go much further than this. If we stop here, the Book of Jonah tells a tale which is alien to us.

The connection between the two parts of the story is not fortuitous nor forced; it is prophetic. There is no other way of seeing any signification in the whole (and it has one), because in human life it is not true that the salvation of a town, even less so that of the world, depends on one man's attitude before God. This man would have to have a unique quality for this to be true. In truth he would not be different from God. The reference in all this is to Jesus Christ. And this third prophecy displays the connection between the life, death, and resurrection of Jesus Christ and the life, death, and resurrection of all the men he came to save. It is in effect from Christ's link with the world that the link between Jonah and Nineveh draws its truth. He had to go down into death in order that those who are there should not be hopelessly delivered up to Satan and in order that those whose death is spiritual might repent. If he is not the first to go, nothing can be done. He also has to come forth from death by resurrection in order that all men might follow him. He has to enter into grace and

102

pardon in order to be the first in these things. The bond is that of Adam and all men in perdition, but it is also that between Jesus Christ and all men in the salvation which is accomplished here.

The objection naturally arises that Jonah is not Jesus Christ, but we have dealt with this already. It must be emphasized, however, that in order to support the objection one cannot argue that Jonah was a sinner and Jesus was without sin. For we must not forget that precisely to link our fate with his Jesus was made sin for us (2 Corinthians 5:21).

On all sides, then, there arises the great edifice which, far from being the plaything of history and human inventions, is solidly calculated and oriented and patiently constructed, which makes no sense except in its crown and head, and which denotes from every angle the unique one who is attended by many generations of those who perform their tasks without knowing they are prophetic, he who is both Savior and Lord, and who reveals to each, and concerning each, what he was in reality.

This is why the Book of Jonah is left unfinished. It ends with the last question which God puts to Jonah. Jonah does not answer. Naturally it is disappointing for us not to know whether Jonah finally understood. Did he reply in humility and adoration, or did he turn his back a last time? In reality Jonah could not reply, for this question is the question of the life and death of the world and not that of the salvation of Jonah. He could not answer this question, and the question is thus put to each of us, no doubt, but the real reason is that it awaited its answer from another.

The Book of Jonah has no conclusion, and the final question of the book has no answer, except from the one who realizes the fulness of the mercy of God and who factually and not just mythically accomplishes the salvation of the world.